HODGES
Orchard Farm
Ashflats Lane
STAFFORD ST18 9BP

A SEASON IN ST PETERSBURG

A SEASON IN ST PETERSBURG

Everyday Life in Changing Russia

JENNY ROBERTSON

A LION BOOK

Copyright © 1994 Jenny Robertson

The author asserts the moral right
to be identified as the author of this work

Published by
Lion Publishing plc
Sandy Lane West, Oxford, England
ISBN 0 7459 3015 8
Albatross Books Pty Ltd
PO Box 320, Sutherland, NSW 2232, Australia
ISBN 0 7324 0852 0

First edition 1994

A catalogue record for this book is available
from the British Library

Printed and bound in Great Britain
by HarperCollins Manufacturing, Glasgow

To Stuart, my fellow traveller

Contents

THE FIRST SNOW

MID-WINTER

THE ADVENT OF SPRING

BLEAK SPRING

1

A Room with a View

'Here's where we're going to live.' My husband Stuart nodded his fur-capped head towards a dirty building. 'It's falling apart, but never mind.'

We were in St Petersburg, on the same latitude as southern Shetland. It was mid-February, bleak but not freezing. If anyone had asked this West of Scotland man to live in a tumbledown building in Lerwick he'd have said, 'No way!' not 'Never mind!'

But 'never mind' is the key to survival here.

We were loaded like Sherpas starting the ascent to Everest, each with a twenty-odd kilo bag across our shoulders, dragging huge suitcases, and juggling cardboard boxes. The string of one was cutting across my hand. We sweated in our heavy coats, having hauled all this stuff over filthy pavements, onto overcrowded public transport, through underpasses, up and down escalators. But: never mind.

I moaned all the same. 'I can't carry this case another step!'

'Come on. It's only across the road,' Stuart said, encouragingly.

Stuart is not usually a stoic. The actor in him sometimes reacts over-dramatically to ups and downs. But Russian life shows he knows how to endure.

Stuart was swaddled in an Arctic patrolman's coat (black simulated leather with an enormous crinkly fur collar) that he'd bought in the Army and Navy Stores. It was definitely for snowy wastes, not for the crowded Underground.

(The rabbit-fur hat he bought last November when it turned cold in St Petersburg was too hot to wear. A pity. I like him in it. He looks good. I told him so, but he discarded it for a horrible check cap our son found bobbing along the Water of Leith one windy day and brought back home for a joke.)

I was elegant in musquash—a gift, like so much of what we carried.

I flexed my muscles and woman-handled my load across a slushy road, weaving between decrepit lorries spraying muddy water. We pushed open the heavy black door of the building Stuart had pointed out, (in need of paint like everything else here). I stood guard in a dark hallway while Stuart went off to find Boris, in whose Society we were going to live and work. People in heavy coats and inevitable rabbit-fur hats stomped purposefully through the building. Stolid Soviet citizens.

They left the door open, letting heat escape.

I kept shutting it. My futile effort at *perestroika*, attempting to 'restructure' a society where no one cares if they waste someone else's heat, stand in someone else's space, slam doors in someone else's face.

I wondered why these pedestrians were using the hallway as a through route. I found out later: these are the builders of the metro, who have their office on the top floor of the left-hand wing of our building.

'They also serve who only stand and wait.' So I hung around until Stuart eventually reappeared with Boris, who welcomed me in his quick Russian. 'We're putting you on the top floor,' he said.

We picked up the bags. I trailed up two flights of stairs after the men, half-hearing, quarter-understanding what Boris said. 'There's a toilet along your corridor. You'll have to go down to the ground floor for the shower.'

He opened a door at the top of the stairs and led us along a wooden-floored corridor. A dark passage with many doors opened out to the right.

'We hope to have lecture rooms and college courses along here in the autumn... There's no kitchen, but you can use the canteen,'

Boris was explaining. 'Here, in here,' he went on, unlocking the second door, on the left-hand side.

So there it was. A south-facing room with wood panelling (mice run over the top), drab wallpaper, a table, chairs. And a view. A room with a view. In this city of tower blocks where windows gleam like lit Christmas trees in the long winter dark we were being given a room with a view. Our windows look over a muddy courtyard, tall thin trees, forbidding brick walls, a golden dome.

And not just one room, but two—connected by an adjoining door. And the balcony... to string up wet washing when warmer weather comes, and even a cramped place to sit, a ledge two feet by four hanging precariously out over the cracks which score the middle of the building.

We put down our bags. Boris showed us along the corridor where he hoped college students would soon be studying. 'Here's the toilet. And the sink. You may get hot water if you run it long enough. Now, is there anything else you need?'

'A toilet seat, perhaps...' I hazarded. Stuart relayed the message to Boris. 'No problem. I'll tell Lena,' Boris said, airily.

Lena, of course, was his wife. In this society men do the talking—and drinking—and women look after the business of living. (And in the shops men sell all the latest electrical goods; women stand along the same counter and sell enamel kitchenware.)

A woman in a white overall came and wiped our lino with a cloth wrapped round a broom.

'It's my first day,' she said. 'I'm on a pension. I've just started back at work. Everything's new.'

I felt exactly the same as I watched her swill dirty water around the floor—and longed for a scrubbing brush, a foam mop, all those familiar western cleansing aids aimed to 'give your home a better shine'.

I fished a packet of rose-hip tea bags out of my luggage—and thereafter she smiled whenever we met.

We started to unpack in our rooms with a view.

We were testing the bed-settee in the inner room for hardness when quick, determined footsteps sounded along the corridor. Lena, Boris' wife looked in at our open door. 'You wanted this,' she said, holding out a toilet seat.

I followed her along the corridor. She plonked the seat down and disappeared. I had a strong feeling that some other lavatory in the building had been denuded of its seat, and ever after, whenever I saw one of her many children I wondered guiltily if I'd deprived the family of a little comfort...

So we began to settle into St Petersburg.

St Petersburg is enthusiastically billed by package holiday brokers as the 'Romantic City of the Tsars'. This northern city, which boasts some of Europe's finest buildings, rose out of swamps inhabited by mosquitoes and Finns—Ingrian people who were colonized and all but absorbed into Russia.

The mosquitoes have never been colonized. We were soon to discover that they come zinging in and bite whenever the temperature rises above freezing.

It's because of the mud and all the canals. Councillors advised Peter the Great not to build his new capital city in the unhealthy marshes at the head of the Gulf of Finland. But Peter, great in ambition as well as stature (he was 6ft 7in), needed an opening to the sea, to the wider world. Having gone to Amsterdam and Greenwich and acquired the skills of shipbuilding and navigation—climbing the rigging with calloused hands like any other sailor—the energetic Tsar came back to whip thousands of serfs into the mud to build his great port, shave the beards off his *boyars* (noblemen) and drag his Asiatic, conservative nation into the late seventeenth century—just as old-style Communists today are being dragged into a capitalism they understand as little as the *boyars* understood razors.

So here we were, caught up in the process of change. Two of the many foreigners who come to do business of all kinds in Russia. Business people, athletes, artists, musicians, evangelists, and, of course, language students, come and go. But we stay.

That's the thing which most surprises Russians, especially

that I am here to stay—a woman from that never-never land they call, in spite of all my protestations, Anglia. That land of gentility, as they think, not having caught up with writers more modern than Galsworthy. Agatha Christie appears in Russian on bookstalls nowadays, and I noticed Georgette Heyer the other day— but neither is the best of sources for an up-to-date picture of life in post-Thatcher Britain.

When the penny finally drops that I'm from *Scotland* people's enchantment grows: misty Scotland, the land of Mary Stewart, Ossian and Walter Scott floats somewhere in the Russian imagination. The Russian word *'skot'* means 'cattle', as the modern poet Joseph Brodsky has pointed out, none too kindly. However, Walter Scott's name is mentioned with bated breath. For Russians he was one the most popular novelists of the nineteenth century. His romantic novels influenced Russian architecture, Russian furniture, so that the writer Gogol said, 'Through the all-powerful words of Walter Scott, who shook the dust from Gothic architecture and showed the world its glory, a taste for everything Gothic spread quickly everywhere and influenced everything...'

No wonder people are surprised that we have left our supposed Gothic castle to come to post-Soviet Russia.

'Why?' people ask us.

'Well...' we try, unsuccessfully, to explain.

It's just as hard back in Britain.

'What do you *do*?' people not unnaturally wonder.

'Learn Russian,' I say, 'and teach English.'

Five million people live in St Petersburg and they all seem to want to learn English. Worse still, they all seem to want me to teach them—or their niece or their son or... In fact, I feel as if wear a label: 'Genuine Native English Speaker'.

'You don't want me,' I complain. 'You only want my tongue.' ('Tongue' and 'language' are the same word in Russian.) 'Nonsense,' they all tell me. 'But, you see...' And I know what's coming next '... I've never met a Native English Speaker before.'

I say, 'But I haven't left my home and family *just* to teach English.' Or be an advocate for British culture.

We have come here in order to open up the Bible in a land where it was officially forbidden for seventy years. A land once called Holy Russia, on which atheism was forcibly imposed. It has been pointed out that more martyrs perished for the faith in the middle of the twentieth century than in the whole two thousand years of Christian history. (The other 'People of the Book'—Muslims and, above all, Jews—suffered too.)

But since English is what everyone wants, I teach two classes, one with ten children, the other with eight, in the school run by our penniless Russian Orthodox Society. (Religious-philosophical, it's rather optimistically called—it's just one of many similar groups which mushroomed with the new freedom of speech at the end of the eighties.)

There are no proper blackboards. The ones we use are brown and cracked and nothing shows. There is no proper chalk. Soviet chalk is faint and powdery. There are no textbooks. However, I don't have far to go to work. One class actually meets at the end of our corridor. We hear their histrionic form teacher screaming at them. She's a mathematician, a brilliant academic who feels, over-enthusiastically, that this school is the Only Hope for Russia, that it is too wonderful to have two English people—actually living in her building—and please, I must help her with her English, as well as teaching the children.

The other class meets in the left-hand wing of the building across the yard that we see from our window, together with the trees (still bare of leaves) and the gleam of gold from the tower of the Cathedral dedicated to Alexander Nevsky, a Russian princely soldier-saint who led invading Swedish armies onto thin ice on 5 April 1242—a clever tactic, bringing Mother Russia's treacherous thaw to the defence of her daughters and her sons.

It's not the Russian snow which defeats foreigners, however. It's the Russian mud.

Here, in St Peterburg, these raw months of a season I usually call spring, I can well believe it. We drown in mud. Everyone brings it in on their shoes. I try vainly to scrub it from those endless corridors, paddling through soap-sudsy water from the weekly wash, which I do in the tiny sink, heating water on an electric ring in our room.

The Russian mud. Even Western detergents can't drive it away.

'What do you do?' The answer is I wash: clothes, dishes, floors, myself; heating and carrying water. The simplest things of life become time-consuming here. No wonder Russian women look at me in amazement! But I live like royalty compared with my women friends.

Water comes yellow from the tap. Once I left a towel lying soaking under running water. The brown stain has never yet come off.

So we do a weekly wash; at least, I wash and Stuart comes and wrings the clothes dry. We have a long wash ourselves, too, downstairs in the shower, running down two flights of stairs in shower robes, shivering as the metro workers come stolidly through the hallway, leaving the door open as usual. Then the blessedness of hot water, the warmth of steam...

So what I have come to know of St Petersburg is rather different from the glitter of opulent theatres, the splendid ballet and opera performances Western visitors see, the guided tours from the comfort of well-heated buses. Although I occasionally visit the Hermitage Museum (once the Tsar's Winter Palace) whose vast façade dominates the banks of the River Neva, it's really to see my friend Nadezhda who works there and—guess what—wants help with her English.

The Winter Palace is the centre of St Petersburg. It was built by a French architect, Rastrelli, who came to St Petersburg as a boy in 1716 with his sculptor father. It's thanks to Rastrelli's genius that the fairytale Baroque palaces and churches of the Russian Tsars became the wonder of Europe. It was said of him that he could transform stone to foam. He managed to adapt the traditional Russian architecture he noted in Moscow to the requirements of Baroque, of Western Europe. The Winter Palace was his last major work, built at a time when the Baroque style was already losing its influence. But under Rastrelli the old form has all the harmony of a Bach cantata.

The Palace, with its one thousand and fifty rooms, one thousand, nine hundred and forty-five windows, magnificently houses the art treasures of the world.

I always ask Nadezhda to let me look at the rich collection of Rembrandts. The flowers on his wife Sasski's headdress glow as brightly as if they had been painted yesterday; the Prodigal kneels, one bare heel exposed, while Christ is taken from the cross above the heads of tourists, and David sends his loyal military commander, Uriah, unsuspectingly away to the battlefield, guilt writ large on the monarch's face.

Nadezhda likes Titian. We look at repentant Magdalene, her upturned eyes luminous with tears, at St Sebastian, shot through with arrows. As we walk through long corridors to spread our English books out in a little-visited gallery full of rather austere Greek nudes, I get a glimpse of a room full of Rodin. But Nadezhda, walking with the swinging grace of a girlhood spent on skates, hurries purposefully on. I glance around wistfully and scuttle behind her.

For I am all the time aware that Nadezhda, who works amongst these treasures, these sumptuous rooms and splendid corridors each with its own theme and style (one, for instance, is copied tile by tile from a corridor in the Vatican), lives with her husband and three young daughters in a single room on the tenth floor of a high-rise block of flats, travelling home in the mad stampede of the overcrowded metro and a single filthy bus, sharing a kitchen and bath with uncouth neighbours—and that the family of five have no beds.

Further down the river-bank stands the original modest palace built by Peter the Great. A corner of the façade is scraped back to show the original brick. At right angles to the Palace runs Millionaire's Street (so called because only the very rich could live here), lined with imposing mansions. And at the end of the street stands the amazing Marble Palace, built by Rastrelli's successor on the orders of Catherine the Great as a gift to one of her lovers, Gregory Orlov. Its severe classical lines are softened by translucent marble, radiating gentle colour in this city of long dark winters and brief summers of endless light.

An angel stands high on a column in the middle of the square in front of the Winter Palace. To this square, on Sunday 9 January 1905, hungry people crowded in meek procession, behind priests with Christ, his mother and all the saints embroidered on their banners, to beg Tsar Nicholas II, the acknowledged father of their holy nation, for bread, for a just government, for the separation of church and state.

Nicholas turned gunfire upon the working people of St Petersburg, thereby anticipating his own downfall. I often think—if the Tsar had listened then to the people, had given them justice, maybe there would still be a royal family in the Winter Palace today. But blood begets blood and the murders wrought by the Tsar's soldiers that day produced the Revolution and the slaughter of the last of the Romanovs.

Nadezhda says, 'I cross this Square every day. I get such comfort from the angel. I'm sure I'm being protected.'

She's the great-granddaughter of a Georgian princess. Her daughters are stunning beauties. I've watched their unspeakable living conditions age Nadezhda. I know that single room is driving her family apart.

So our days go by. Stuart sometimes helps me with the teaching in the school. He interprets and translates day and night for the flow of foreign visitors who pass through our building. And he sits hour-long at the seminars the forty or so members of the Society take very seriously, attend assiduously. They're all men, apart from the secretary, a physicist. They sit on hard stools and philosophize in quick, intellectual, muttered Russian. It always amazes me that this nation of singers, who declaim poetry, screeds of it, are so bad at public speaking. Perhaps it comes from years of enforced attendance at propaganda meetings.

The Soviet Union was like a single sprawling overcrowded room. A room with only one view: its own glory. The rest of the world could be glimpsed literally 'as through a glass, darkly'.

People had to read between the lines of cheap newsprint, listen to jammed radio programmes, snatch forbidden books whose dust jackets were kept carefully covered. (You read such books late at night, peering from time to time anxiously over one shoulder, sensing almost physically the noose about your neck.) The wonder is that some Russians know so much, have read so widely the forbidden literature of the wider world.

These men who sit on hard stools have all been drop-outs. Some indeed have known what it's like to be followed, spied on, arrested, have even endured the Gulag. They don't know what a regular working week is. They have no qualifications as we understand the term.

I find their endless muttering incredibly self-indulgent.

'There's a lecture on Shakespeare tonight,' Stuart tells me. 'You should go.'

'I'm not going,' I tell him. 'I can't understand it, and anyway I've got school work to prepare for tomorrow. And Russian grammar.'

I say exactly the same thing every Sunday, too. 'I can't understand it...' Only this time it's not muttered Russian. It's something even worse. It's Finnish—because the Finnish-speaking Ingrian people who were all but colonized by Russia are trying to recover their culture, their language and their church life. Stuart has been asked to help them.

He finds he's been made sole pastor of a Lutheran church out of town. To begin with I went with him. It was good to leave crowded city streets, to be out among trees and wooden houses, away from communal flats and tower blocks, to see pussy willow opening on frosty branches, to breathe what seems like purer air—though we're one railway stop from a nuclear power station which leaks.

The church was once a beautiful building, overlooking the blue glitter of the Gulf of Finland. My heart would lift at the sight of the sea—and sink at the dereliction in which Stuart works each Sunday, preaching in Russian and leading prayers and hymns in Finnish.

19

Under Stalin the building was used as a cinema. Old cinema posters now vainly feed a single stove which gives no heat, in what is euphemistically called the pastor's vestry. Stuart wears as much as he can and dons a long, black cloak, but the material is almost transparently thin.

The cavernous, freezing church is crowded out with elderly peasant women, whose native language had been banned by the Soviets. (Religion was forbidden in any case, but things became particularly dangerous for the Ingrian people when neighbouring Finland stood out against the mighty Soviet Empire in the Winter War.) Stalin deported the Ingrians to the Gulag. Many of the women in Stuart's congregation lost their sons and husbands there. Others spent their girlhood in the labour camps. Now they travel miles to come to a church service in Finnish. Younger people, who are trying to recover their destroyed culture, come to church because there they can hear the language their parents refused to let them learn—it was too dangerous.

Coming from Scotland where Scots and Gaelic are experiencing a revival, we cannot but be sympathetic. The simple fact is: the Ingrian folk want their services to be held not in Russian, but in the Finnish which was forbidden for so long.

Two candles glow between a wooden cross on a table, pale in the gloom of the building. Water freezes to the inside of the walls. Stuart's hands freeze too, glued to the pages of the prayer book. Stuart can praise the Lord in very passable Finnish; asking for a cup of coffee is a bit harder. Luckily—and incongruously in this area of ramshackle wooden houses, most of them used only as *dachas* (summer houses), without piped water or sanitation—coffee is always available, supplied by bus-loads of visiting Finns, along with electric coffee makers, connected precariously to antiquated wall plugs. There are no other conveniences, which poses problems for the pastor, being away from home from 7.45a.m. till 4p.m. every Sunday.

After going once or twice, I opted out. 'I can't,' I protested weakly. 'I don't have the energy, not after a week teaching, learning Russian, struggling out to my teacher's flat on those awful buses. Besides, the prayers and hymns are all in Finnish.'

So I go weekly to the Orthodox cathedral whose domes we see from our window. The bells ring for service. I put on my headscarf and walk round the corner, down an avenue past the sellers of over-priced souvenirs and icons, past the beggars, past the entrance to the cemetery where St Petersburg's greatest composers and writers are buried: Tschaikovsky, Borodin, Rimsky-Korsakov, Mussorgsky. And Dostoyevsky.

The text from the Gospel of John, chapter 12 which begins *The Brothers Karamazov* is engraved on his grave: 'Except a grain of wheat falls into the ground and dies it remains alone...'

In the days when the Bible was forbidden that verse remained, indelibly, ineradicably there. I first saw Dostoyevsky's grave one bitter January day some years ago. We'd been to his house, which is now a museum where the curator still puts a fresh glass of strong tea each day on the dead writer's desk.

And on his grave I found a single red tulip, frozen in the snow.

I never dreamt, then, that I'd be living permanently only a stone's throw away.

Or that I'd stand among the Orthodox, old and young, for as many hours as I can endure in the warm glow of candlelight, amid the flashbulbs of tourists' cameras, and hear the chanting of the choirs.

No, I cannot go along the railway line with Stuart, sit listening to a language I cannot understand, while the cold seeps in through my boots, through every layer of clothing right to the very marrow of my bones.

But now there are dramas and fights and bawlings out in our Society.

First of all the metro builders start insisting that our Society has no right to occupy the building. I hear shouts and scuffles. Things almost come to blows. The front door gets barricaded with huge blocks of wood to keep the metro workers out. We have to squeeze through a broken-down fence at the far side of the building and pick our way over a sea of mud into the backyard.

Next it's panic stations. There's going to be a conference with visiting Dutch Christians. The theme will be the Reformation—a topic almost unheard of in Russia. But the present pressing need is a practical one.

'If you're going to run an international conference centre you must provide proper facilities,' the Dutch have said. 'We'll help you all we can, but it's up to you to get the place ready.'

They do indeed help. They provide carpets—and people in the Society insist we have a left-over bit for our main floor. Our bed-settee becomes a real bed thanks to two mattresses provided by the same generous folk. Holland is a small nation where people have big hearts.

Big hearts, indeed. One man came from Amsterdam for a planning weekend prior to the conference. He decided to set up a fund to bring prostitutes to Holland—not I should hasten to explain, to join the women already working in the red-light districts in Amsterdam, but to have a chance of a different way of life.

Finding our place a bit too low-grade he took up residence in the hotel across the road and evangelized the girls in the currency bars. He kindly invited us across for a bath in his *en suite* bathroom—we forgot to take a plug with us, but four tumblers in the plug hole reduced the outflow to a mere seepage! I haven't heard any more about the 'Ludmilla campaign', but we enjoyed our soak.

Meantime, to fulfil the Dutch requirements workmen invade the corridor.

Our single toilet gets uprooted and sits abjectly in the corridor. We still have the sink with a cold tap where we stand ankle-deep in cement and plaster, then trample the stuff all through our rooms. I give up trying to wash the floors.

In the middle of this some Finnish students from a Mission College arrive. They stay along the corridor and eat all their meals with us. They are serious young people, bent on giving out tracts as we travel together on overcrowded public transport. Stuart and I tend to feel faith can't be meaningfully compressed into a few lines of print, especially in Russia.

'You have to earn the right to be heard,' Stuart suggests as they chauffeur him in a borrowed car to Lutheran churches in outlying areas, across roads reminiscent of the battlefields of the Somme. 'It's not just a matter of learning to speak Russian: you have to learn about the culture here—and you can't ignore all the rich traditions of Orthodoxy.'

They don't agree but they are good-hearted young people who endure the cold in Stuart's church where the seats shake with our collective, juddering shivers. As we wave them away we feel the students Stuart teaches here could learn a lot from their unselfish commitment.

But there are soon plenty of new distractions. The histrionic mathematics teacher comes screaming along the corridor. Lena, Boris' wife, has just announced that the class must vacate its room at the end of our corridor. 'And go into the other wing where there's no room for them at all,' the teacher adds. 'Foreign visitors—that's all Lena and Boris think about,' she accuses, unjustly. 'Western money! I'm resigning.'

Which she does. The Only Hope for Russia has to manage without her, after all.

Another teacher is found. We soon discover it's too typical. 'Hire and fire,' Stuart says grimly.

Meantime mosquitoes keep biting, and I get bad reactions.

'It's because you keep on scratching those bites,' Stuart tells me.

'I can't help it,' I protest. 'They itch.' And I asphyxiate us both by burning mosquito coils which should be used only out in the open, at the barbeque or campfire. The kids and I do a clean-up in the school. We discover an empty room: a huge poster of Lenin conceals what turns out to be a large, filthy bath.

Four days to go to the conference. The workmen are found stone drunk in an empty room. So they get fired too.

It's action stations now. We all wash floors, carry furniture. Everyone who has a friend who knows someone gets roped in to help. Boris's three teenage sons work all night.

A bath gets carried along our corridor—to the classroom

which the kids have been turned out of.

I go to have a look.

'I think I've seen that bath before somewhere,' I tell Stuart. 'It can't be...'

But it is: the filthy bath we found underneath the poster of Lenin. It is yellowed from years of dirty water, its enamel is chipped away, and now it graces what has become a tiled bathroom. There's even a shower too.

It's the same along the other end. Our toilet has been put back, and another one built in...

The conference begins. A Korean evangelist has somehow joined the Dutch team. He gets up to preach after breakfast in the canteen one morning, shouting as though he's in Seoul stadium. We have a three-way translation, from Korean into Russian, by an interpreter he's brought with him, and from Russian into English for the benefit of the fluent Dutch.

The preacher goes on—and on, trapping the ladies in the kitchen who want to come out and clear the tables, but don't dare step into the line of fire. The rest of us have no escape either. Someone pointedly looks at his watch.

'You have all eternity to burn in hell,' the evangelist declares in fierce Korean, 'so why grudge a minute now in which you might be saved.' His voice rises to a shout, making us all jump and even startling the cat, curled up on a bench beside us.

On the whole the conference was a success. Even though it plainly showed there were huge differences between Protestant and Orthodox it was, as one man put it, good not to pretend these differences don't exist.

We waved our guests away. Overwhelmed by floods of preaching, the Russians immediately opened up some vodka. I went upstairs to soak my weary self on broken enamel in a deep, deep, hot (if rust-coloured) bath.

Then it was our own turn to say goodbye. True to Russian custom we sat with Boris and Lena amongst our packing cases for a moment's silence before we took our leave. I'm sure no one expected we'd come back.

Our bags much lighter than when we'd arrived (even though thirty- six people had given us letters, postcards and small parcels to post 'from outside'), we stood on an uncovered platform on Finland Station, waiting for the train to open its doors and carry us away. The first real snow of the bleak season I can no longer call spring started to fall in thick, full flakes. It was Maundy Thursday.

In Russia it was going to be a white Easter.

So we travelled back to Scotland, where I was to stay for the rest of the summer, packing up the remnants of our former Edinburgh life, and trying not to forget the Russian I had so painstakingly acquired, ready for a more permanent return.

INDIAN SUMMER

2

The Goldfish Bowl

While I remained in sunless Edinburgh, packing twenty-seven years of married life into boxes to be stowed in the lofts of family and friends, Stuart was back in St Petersburg.

It was the season of White Nights, the six weeks of May and June when this northern city experiences endless light. People book midnight cruises up and down the River Neva, along the network of canals which gives the city its name as the Venice of the North.

At 2a.m. it's light enough to read a paper, so it didn't matter too much that there was no electricity in our building. The metro builders who'd caused a few hassles earlier in the year were trying another take-over bid of the building. Physical threats having done little, they cut the power cable, trying to squeeze our Society out that way.

But life in St Petersburg today consists of doing without. Boris rigged up an illegal cable, so some sort of cooking could be done. Stuart got a cooked lunch of sorts, though for five weeks he wasn't able to boil a kettle. He survived on tepid tea made from water the night watchman brought him in that mainstay of Russian life, a thermos flask. This watchman was a gentle young man with soft eyes, very typically Russian. Like many, he had a traditional sort of animistic belief in the spirits. He left to go back to the pine forests and talk to the trees.

Eventually fathers and sons, uncles and nephews—and

Stuart—dug up the mud in the backyard and laid another electric cable.

Stuart came back to Edinburgh in July an extremely long-suffering man with blisters on his hands—Soviet spades end in a point, not a handle. (He made sure he packed a spade with a handle in the luggage we sent by sea.)

We returned to St Petersburg in early September to find green leaves on the trees. I'd never seen this city softened by green; but everything was parched after the long, dry summer.

We unpacked our cases in our rooms with a view. The other three rooms and bathroom our end of the corridor are euphemistically called 'The Hotel'. The bath in particular is not quite hotel standard—it's the one we found in the clean-up of the school. Stuart has brought enamel paint to try to improve its pitted, stained surface. So poor is Russian grout and, sad to say, so shoddy was the workmanship in the mad rush to get the bathroom ready, that tiles regularly fall off the walls with a crashing noise. Things that go bump in the night... We have to explain it's nothing to worry about to the guests who come and go. For we have become rather like unofficial wardens, providing tea or coffee day and night. Milk and something to eat is a bit more problematic.

So is the phone. Ours is a communal one, shared by everyone else all over the building. It rings incessantly, but it's seldom for us. Receiving calls is fraught with difficulty; visitors who want to borrow our phone can have a long wait on our settee before they get through.

Our life here is lived always under the public eye. So the moment of our arrival, before we'd even started unpacking, Lena, the director of 'our' school, came along to invite us over for a cup of tea and to bring us up to date with their news.

Her husband Boris had been to conferences in America and Switzerland, his first ever visits to the West. He told us how ex-Communists have jumped on the bandwagon of religion. One delegate inadvertently slipped into the old jargon. 'As Marx says... er, er, Christ.' God is in—but so are the old brigade.

They've changed their coats but there's been no real conversion. There was a film which shook Russia in the eighties. It was called *Pokayanie*—'repentance'. But that cannot come if people merely pay lip-service to newly permitted expressions of belief.

With that sober thought we went back to our rooms, crossing the yard in which rustling plane trees thrust up to the short-lived summer. The door rasped across the carpeted floor. We looked back to the golden dome of the Cathedral, caught in the last light of the dying day. We share the feeling, up in our two rooms, of being like monks in a cell. It's poor and shabby, but this venture isa work of faith, even if relationships in the Society with which we live and work are strained. There are cracks in the building, all right, but we are beginning to understand that there are cracks in the very fabric of society—our own Society and the wider one as well.

Visitors come with smiles and enthusiasm. We may complain about life in the West but it's so pre-packed and gift-wrapped that we can easily use it to mask the bad spots; we can soften our lives. Here, life is lived in the raw. People smoking their guts out, knocking back the vodka.

The new thing is the adverts; consumerism reigns. Adverts for Western cigarettes are blazoned over the walls of the metro which until now have been bare. Except that this whole country was once one vast advertisement for Marxism-Leninism. The undergound stations were built like palaces to proclaim with mosaics, statues, slogan, even their very names, the glories of the new workers' state. They are all oh, so tawdry now. This country is still in the fifties—still in the Dark Ages, some would say.

'Russia needs a firm hand,' said one old Communist. 'We need a leader.' There are plenty of people who lament the passing of the disciplined life of earlier days when transport and bread were cheap and you saw no beggars on the streets. The day after our arrival we travel by metro where people seem to be endlessly going round and round in a goldfish bowl. The sides used to be dark. Few could see out. Now the glass is clear, but exit is harder than ever, as the value of the rouble spirals ever down. The trouble with living in an aquarium is that the view of the world outside is always distorted.

I glance at the people around me. The old woman opposite could have been in the slum clearance area where I grew up in the fifties: dried-out perm, haggard face, faded crimplene, a beaten, broken, exhausted piece of flotsam.

We change at a central point, travel two stops to Alexander Nevsky Square, our station. There's a long, slow ride up the escalator here. On the down-going escalator a middle-aged couple topple, too drunk to stand. An elderly woman reproves them. The woman in an official red hat who sits on guard in her box at the bottom, keeping the comrades in order, stops the down escalator. These women, who are paid a pittance to sit and stare hour-long at the endless flow of humanity up and down the escalators, are somehow symptomatic of the emptiness of life here. They're supposed to represent law and order. Little do the powers that be realize how the presence of these women shocks foreigners even more than the beggars who now congregate round every public place.

We cross the square, the ill-lit main street. I say to Stuart, 'This is the main road of the second city of the Soviet Union—and look at it: dim lights, hardly any traffic, rutted road...'

We collapse into bed, sleep late. I have an unusually vivid dream. I know I'm experiencing my feelings at having gone away from home, missing those encounters when grown-up kids dash in for food and offload washing, together with a few crumbs of their lives.

Stuart goes downstairs for breakfast. It is being served in the dining-room or canteen where we usually eat lunch with the schoolchildren, because there are foreign visitors. Six French women teachers—one of them, I think, a nun—have come for a couple of weeks, and when there are visitors here the hospitality of the canteen gets extended to us, too.

But I stay in bed. Bells ring from the Alexander Nevsky Lavra Church, whose domes we see each time we look out of our window. Is it a feast day? Flies buzz. I long for prayer, for God.

I've been reading the biography of Thomas Merton. All summer I've been haunted by Merton's words about dark city-centre churches where you can kneel and pray in peace. All summer I've passed the unlocked doors of the Cathedral, and gone instead to the temple of commerce next door, the shopping centre.

The path for Thomas Merton lay through monasticism, silence. But that's on bended knees in church. How about in daily life? Here? It may well be that the way of penitence, *pokayanie*, is the way of joy, simplicity, of innocence, even. How does it work out for a married woman?

I think of my dream of home and remember how people used to make long sea journeys 'out' to some country which was recognizably 'abroad'. A three-hour flight has whisked us away to another world. Stuart can make the change. He always has been able to. After he's been abroad, even for lengthy periods, he slots back into life at home, and you'd never know he'd so completely changed his language, his way of life. I can't do it. My spirit still needs to catch up.

Merton quotes a Hindu monk who says Christian missionaries had so little impact in India because they always lived so far apart from the 'natives'. How about here? Hotels and dollar shops are affordable to us, if we choose. But not to our Russian friends.

I'm caught napping. I'm still not dressed when there's a knock at the door.

It's a formal deputation: a visit from the wives of the captain and mate of a ship stranded in Leith docks. We're trying to help them join their husbands (unsuccessfully, it turned out in the end). They bring flowers. They're wearing their best clothes ... I escape into our inner room and pull on a thin black trouser suit I bought in a catalogue sale. It's hot today. Flies buzz round, annoyingly. We pour tea, coffee, offer biscuits, talk about their planned visit to Edinburgh, the problems they're having with visas, with life here.

'We can't understand what's happening in our country,' they say. 'We used to have *poryadok* (order), safety.'

How hard it is to explain that the disciplined lifestyle which kept trouble off the streets was corrupt, that so-called order was bought at the price of freedom, that perhaps the changes are for the better—when things are so plainly falling apart. And in any case, my tongue ties itself in knots as I talk!

The spiralling rate of inflation means that women like these navy wives, who used to be fairly comfortably off, now find themselves paupers, and their husbands, caught up in a quarrel between shipping companies, have no means of knowing when they will get home.

Back in Edinburgh, Stuart was honorary chaplain in the port of Leith. He'd been going on board Soviet ships for years, long before such things were possible officially (there still is no Christian presence in any Russian workplace or place of learning, though clergy now visit prisons). Stuart's fluent Russian, his understanding of Soviet mentality gave him ready access to the ships. He was welcomed aboard with the words: '*Pastor prishol*—the pastor's here.' An absolute irony in the days when pastors and priests were still confined to the worst places of the Gulag...

When I was back in Edinburgh last May I readily agreed to go aboard the clapped-out vessel which had carried rape-seed from Szczeczin in Poland across the North Sea. Igor, the captain, shook my hand in amazement and said: 'Well done!' when he heard I actually lived in St Petersburg.

We realized from the plight of this crew how little the lives of men who serve the ships count in the big business of maritime commerce. Unscrupulous masters work Philippinos and Mauritians, in particular, no better than slaves. They frequently work up to 480 hours a month for only \$150–\$250, living in cramped conditions, often sailing rough seas on small vessels. Russians, with their dire economy, are coming into the same category. In the end these men spent nine months marooned in the port. Igor, the captain, played chess against himself and learnt English to pass the time.

We had entrusted four tea-chests and two trunks of overflow belongings to the goodwill of Igor and his crew. Some of this was personal stuff: kitchenware, extra winter coats and so on. Much of it was gifted: good quality second-hand clothing, toiletries, equipment for the school. Stuart added a spare cassock, his degree hood and scarf.

So we were waiting, too, for the boat to come safely into port in St Petersburg...

The women go, leaving the smell of their perfume in the room, and I sit out on our balcony, trying not to think of the cracks which split the brickwork below me. The sun is mellow. Bars lie in shadows across my legs. I watch two of Lena's boys play in the dust, totally absorbed. The sounds of children at play are international.

How happy I am to have sunshine, a place to sit and enjoy the warmth!

Because the French schoolteachers are still here, food in the canteen is a bit more varied than usual. We eat chicken soup with cream, fish fried with onions, potatoes, tomatoes, cucumbers, prune compote. In the winter, a slice of cucumber will seem like a dream.

The French women are taking showers in cold water. I'm not so brave. I boil a kettle to have a wash in the hand basin, but this is over-optimistic. The plug doesn't fit and the heated water disappears before I can wash both feet.

Another week goes by. Church bells ring again. Stuart goes to a Finnish service out of town, for the ceremonial opening and dedication of a church rebuilt in pine, thanks to Finn-aid. This fine new building must be a glimpse into another world for the women of the congregation. They live without running water in their wooden homes, far less flush toilets and taps which work Finnish-style—hot if you turn the single handle one way, cold the other.

It's another mild day, a real Indian Summer. I recall that the Catholic church building on the main Nevsky Prospekt is supposed to have been given back, and I venture out to investigate. Perhaps there will be a service there for me.

Beggars sit on pavements and around the metro exits. Unwashed children stretch out thin hands. A young man bends, gives coins. I give nothing. The church is closed with no sign of life. It's a beautiful building, standing on the other side of Nevsky Prospekt from the shopping arcade, Gostinny Dvor. Once this arcade was the shopping mall of St Petersburg. It's sadly run down now, but despite the peeling paint, the myriad pieces of paper advertising things to buy and sell, it's still an attractive two-storey building. The shopping arcade and the handsome church, St Catherine's, were both built in the 1760s, the work of the same French architect.

Across the austere classical façade of the church is written in Latin, 'My house shall be called a house of prayer.' The same words, in Slavonic, are written across St Isaac's Cathedral, another handsome St Petersburg church, built on the site of the original wooden cathedral where Peter the Great married his il-literate wife. St Isaac's was used as a museum of religion—inevitably with an anti-religious slant. But it has been given back to be used for worship once more, so it's sad to see that St Catherine's is still closed although friends have assured me that the authorities have given it back. Perhaps it will be opened again soon and the text above its fluted columns will come true.

Artists set out their paintings for sale in the square in front of the church, and there's a queue forming at an ice-cream stall. I cross Nevsky by an underpass, leaving the sunlight for the underground, and ride back home on the metro. Bells chime from the Orthodox church, deep-throated. Church bells were silenced for years, in a country where, as in C.S. Lewis' Narnia, it was 'always winter, and never Christmas'.

It's quiet in the building now. I hear a trickle, a light falling sound, rather like rain, but it isn't. It's the metro. When escalators run beneath us everything shivers and shakes: the cups in the cupboard, the furniture, ourselves. Westerners call this a tumble-down dump. Locals say proudly, 'It's a fine old St Petersburg building.'

It was, however, built only in 1953, and used as communal flats. I know this for a fact because one of our friends seemed to know the building well. When we asked why, he laughed and said he used to date a girl who lived along one of the corridors in the other wing of the building. So whole families shared our toilet and single cold tap until subsidence caused them to be evacuated and the building was left lying empty. Then, in the heady days of *glasnost*, when new freedoms opened up and Utopia seemed within grasp of people who for years had been deluded that their country was building a 'brilliant future', the building was given lock, stock and barrel to our Society.

No other group struggling to start alternative education, to run courses, hold church services, has been given such a gift.

But it has to be repaired, maintained. Underneath the building is a labyrinth—an entire town, people say. All Stalinist buildings had these unlit underground passages as a protection in the event of atomic war. The central heating system is there: the pipes are rotting, and the only way to do any sort of repair is by torchlight.

There are plenty of people in the city who would like to get their hands on this building, and businesses, we're told, would pay a mint just for the site...

So it's a big fight to maintain the building—and a big fight to keep hold of it, requiring hours of hassle, paperwork and careful negotiation with the town council, who keep trying to take their gift back. One of the men who works here says, looking at the cracks in the walls: 'We're in the hands of God.'

Work in school where I teach English goes on. Stuart's kept busy too, teaching New Testament Greek (a subject forbidden for ears) to students who meet along our corridor and who congregate during intervals at the top of our stairs for a smoke.

Foreign visitors stream through, days pass. Somewhere out there, there's a world. And we're here in this goldfish bowl, where five million people endlessly travel on overcrowded buses, trolleys, trams, underground and overground trains, where beggars hold out their hands, their hats, and criminals control charities, the church, everything.

3

Birch Leaves and Honey

The weather's wet now, but it's still warm. I'm not used to so many hours of daylight here.

We are going to see our friend Olga, who boarded and fed us last autumn. We slept on the bed-settee in her living-room, our heads against the freezer which recharged itself noisily; and she stood in five-hour queues to buy our food.

Like so many others, Olga has been housed in the concrete blocks which tower out of mud and dereliction. It's a kind of living nightmare, like the aftermath of a bomb blast. Huge pylons stride across potholed roads without asphalt. The few straggling trees only add to the sense of desolation. There are attempts to make some blocks face away from others, but there's nothing to delight the eye or ease the soul. Some families live without sunlight, constantly cut off from the warm rays of the sun by the remorseless shadows of tall buildings flung across their windows.

A new metro station is being built fairly close to Olga's house. Until that's opened, it's a twenty-minute bus-ride to the metro. Last autumn a single bus served this housing estate of one million people. Now there's a second bus with rows of double seats. It costs more—in fact, the price goes up every month—but it helps reduce the bone-breaking scrum on those yellow, Hungarian-made buses (called Icarus: a nasty misnomer) which used to serve the whole Eastern bloc, with people crowded together like cattle.

Once I decided no one could possibly squeeze onto the over-crowded bus as its doors strained shut upon jam-packed humanity. So I stood back. But when the bus jolted away, I faced the twenty-minute wait for the next bus utterly alone: everyone else had managed to pack themselves on.

The entrance to Olga's first-floor flat is like a slum. But she has spent the summer at her *dacha* away in the north-east, in Karelia, on the far shores of Lake Ladoga, among the Veps (Finnic) people. There her four children, normally walled up in the city without a green leaf or a blade of grass, splash in the river and run among fields. And Olga grows potatoes and fruit to feed them all winter. 'I live like a peasant,' she laughs. 'What can you do? I've got to feed my family.'

Olga feeds us stew, salad, plum preserves, tea with herbs.

She loves her *dacha*—the emptiness, wide spaces—a nine-hour bus ride away, over non-existent roads, winding in and out of every little settlement. And of course, no motorway stops, no cafeteria or conveniences. Everything has to be carried there: spades, the cat, pots and jamjars of seedlings to be planted out, the kids and their clothes, food for the whole family all summer.

'We're on the top of a hill,' she explains. 'Forests all around: real forests with wolves and lynxes. The wolves come into the villages in the autumn, but in summer it's all right. We never see them.'

'There's salmon in the river,' the children say enthusiastically.

It's illegal to catch them, but people do.

'The peasants are good people, true country folk,' Olga says. 'They live off the land. They're self-sufficient—not drunkards or layabouts.' And so that's where we are. Just the sky above us. An arch of blue stretching as far as you can see. Nothing between us and God...

Her husband, an international figure after years in the Gulag, has been away all summer. There are always visitors from abroad, and Olga, one of the few people we know who is without self-seeking, without a single axe of her own to grind, feeds and houses them without complaint. As she did us last autumn.

She carries bags that Stuart, no weakling, finds difficult to lift. She carried such bags across the vast Soviet empire, travelling day and night to visit the husband she was denied all access to. They were granted one meeting when he was first sentenced. And she was stripped and searched—they even parted her lovely thick red hair. Many marriages broke under the pressures of the KGB, the long separations. But Olga married for love, and the memories of those days, fraught with hardship, lit with the love of friends, softens the face of a generous woman who bears the marks of hardship beyond her years.

I remember how we—her children, Olga and I—rubbed salt and honey over each other's backs and shoulders in the Russian baths last year: salt to cleanse, honey—melting immediately in the heat of the sauna—to soften the skin, making redundant my packaged lotions, all subtitled 'real', 'genuine'.

This nation has one great institution which helps everyone survive the pitiless life: the Russian baths. 'A proven relief for stress,' a doctor assured me, seriously.

I'd heard about lots of enthusiastic tales of the *banya*. Stuart had gone once with a friend armed with vodka and sausage—and he got the birch leaf beating. I'd heard stories about running from steaming saunas into freezing water, into snow. So Olga and I went off with the kids and bundles of equipment. It was pouring with rain. The wind whipped around us. We waded through puddles and mud towards a heavy door, in need of a coat of paint, as is everything here. And downstairs to the women's section.

People were already walking around wrapped in sheets. We soon got undressed too, and Olga produced sheets for us all. Three-year-old Vanya didn't want to take off his baptismal cross. But his mother thought the metal would get too hot, so off came crosses and jewellery. On went rubber flip-flops and woolly hats (to protect our hair from the dry heat).

And so into the sauna, a small room, all of wood, with a covered stove in one corner. Olga thought it was a poor sauna, heated only to 80 degrees. But the hot, dry air took my breath away. Women shifted to make room for us. Olga sat Vanya on her knee. No one talked much, and when they did it was in whispers. The heat was all-embracing and the air smelt sweet. I breathed in the warmth, and felt myself relax completely.

Here, truly, in this country of hardship, was something which existed for the comfort and well-being of the people.

I saw what looked like oil gleam on people's bodies. It was sweat, and soon it began to run down our own. Vanya said he'd had enough and his sisters took him outside to the showers. Olga and I settled back, soaked in the sweet-smelling warmth—then out to plunge into a bath of cold, cold water—three times, said Olga, for the Holy Trinity. Vanya got dunked in too, in spite of his howls. Then we crowded under warm showers where women were soaping each other's backs, scrubbing each other with loofahs and sponges. Some people had birch leaves sticking to their wet shoulders, and more leaves floated with soapsuds down the drains.

We soaped ourselves, dried ourselves with our linen sheets, put our hats back on and went into the sauna for a second time— this time with salt to rub into our skin. 'For cleansing,' Olga explained.

Then back through cold water and showers. One rotated, spraying cold water from all sides. Vanya ran in and out of it, laughing with delight. The outside world, with its conflicts and difficulties, seemed far away.

Then, since the Lord, explained Olga, likes everything in threes, we went into the sauna for a third time. And now it was time to open the honey, virtually unobtainable except at exorbitant prices. This was strictly for external use. We rubbed it into one another. There wasn't a hint of stickiness. It melted immediately, softening the skin. Olga massaged her little boy. I'd seen his sister do this too, singing little songs. I thought of our aromatherapy sessions, our alternative medicine, and knew that this age-old system of bathing, with its communal nudity, yet lack of voyeurism (friends and colleagues sit side by side in the *banya*, and still call each other by the formal 'you') is something which offers sanity and health.

And finally into the steam room, where friends switch birch leaves across each other's bodies, fathers and sons in the men's section, mothers and children in the women's.

'It drives disease away,' Olga explained.

The steamy heat was easier to bear than the dry. We didn't go into the cold bath this time, just back under showers for a final soaking.

The whole process had taken two hours. We finished our morning with glasses of herbal tea, and went out into the rain and wind to stand again in the queues for food, and wait for a tram-car home.

Tourists should include a ride on public transport in their itinerary, if they want to see the way people live here. It's a very good way to get into close contact with people. And they should certainly visit the Russian baths—with salt and honey and birch leaves—since the Father likes things in threes.

4

The Metro, Myrrh and a Martial Family

Where would this city be without its metro? Its depth, its efficiency—trains rattle round their circuit every three minutes or so—never fail to impress foreign visitors, though it's not as grand or as large-scale as the Moscow metro. The first underground stations in St Petersburg were built in 1955, temples of Communism, with ornate pillars, bronze victory symbols, for all the world like the spears and wreaths of Roman legionaries. Sculptures show happy peasants with horses, children with doves, workers with smiles, poets and scientists, all builders of the brilliant future most people truly at that time believed in. There are mosaics of Lenin, happy harvesters, writers, slogans proclaiming peace—and Soviet victory.

Some say Stalin built the metro deep for air-raid shelters in event of war. There is still virtually no graffitti; there are no adverts (except the new ones for Western cigarettes); there is no colour. A woman's voice is piped through the system telling citizens how to use the metro: not to run on the escalators, to give way to passengers with children, with white sticks, to the elderly. Nowadays we hear the voice of capitalism: information about what's on sale; about new courses in foreign languages; occultism; hypnotism; quack cures; evangelistic campaigns.

Nowadays, too, beggars and the homeless shelter in the metro. Children sleep, curled on the floor in the dust of many trampling feet. A pauper child kneels upright, eyes lowered, hand held out;

drunks keel and collapse; the police come, called by the uniformed woman who sits in a box at the bottom of the escalators, her face blank from doing nothing, just as women sit hour-long in museums and art galleries, on guard, doing nothing.

Around the entrance to the metro stations we see the beginnings of capitalism. People stand in the street for hours with a pair of shoes, a coat, a fur hat; or with puppies and kittens tucked inside their coats; or packets of cigarettes, bottles of beer, vodka: things they've bought—or acquired—from the state shops and sell at marked-up prices. Next stage up is a stall. Swarthy men from the south burn crates to keep warm in winter: the women stand and sell. The next stage again is a kiosk. Some are lit by candles, others have electric light. People travel to Poland, Turkey, the Baltic States, to buy goods. You can buy cartons of juice, jars of coffee, clothes—all at prices beyond the dream of ordinary Russians—and always with a risk of being cheated.

There have been attempts to keep street sellers away from tourist areas; across the road from us, we've seen police moving sellers of beer away.

'But,' complains one stallholder, correctly, 'we represent capitalism.' Who knows what future chain-store millionaire may not be here? There are thriving businesses in the West which grew out of barrows in the street.

We dodge past the sellers of goods and catch a tram through jerry-built blocks of high-rise buildings on the site of what once was a large aerodrome, very close to the Gulf of Finland. Wind whistles between the concrete buildings, reminding me of Glasgow, whose housing estates fill Russian visitors with horror: it's all too like home.

In the children's playground a few stunted birches and rowans try to give a hint of green. Gulls scream and scavenge round foul-smelling, unemptied refuse bins on waste ground between houses where dogs and children play.

We've been invited to the home of my Russian teacher, Sonia. During the time I've been learning her language we've become friends—and even closer, for she and her husband asked us to be godparents when their sons were baptized last spring, a great privilege for us.

The Orthodox are marvellous at ceremony. Faith is expressed by feasting and fasting, and Russian women are learning the old Russian recipes their great-grandmothers knew before faith was forbidden: recipes for goodies like fragrant Easter cake at Pascha, the greatest festival of all, leaner recipes for Lent when meat, fish, eggs and dairy products are all forbidden. Sonia observed a meatless Lent for the first time this year, though she provided the odd scrawny piece of chicken and heavily breaded meat-balls for the boys, whose baptism was held in the nearest church, a forty-five-minute walk away, set amongst trees and those typical wooden houses I love so much which are being swallowed up by high-rise housing blocks. It was a mid-week ceremony, held after morning prayer in a church still redolent of incense and warm with the glow of many candles.

The boys were given no preparation. Sonia had discovered they might be asked to repeat the Lord's Prayer. This would be hard, especially for ten-year-old Vladik, for the Orthodox prayers are in Old Church Slavonic, a language no one speaks any more.

However, I was able to come to the rescue! One of the results of the haphazard way I've learnt Russian over the years is that although I still get lost over verbs of motion—and much else besides—I can recite the Lord's Prayer in Slavonic. I had even, in a rare moment's forethought, photocopied a few of the prayers with which the Orthodox begin their morning and evening worship, including the Lord's Prayer.

That sheet of photocopied prayers hangs on Sonia's kitchen wall and to hungry Vladik's chagrin we recite our grace and the Lord's Prayer at mealtimes while the soup cools on our plates.

However, the priest didn't ask the boys to recite the prayer. Nor, to our relief, did he ask us, the godparents, if we were Orthodox. I'm afraid he might well have refused to baptize the boys if he had known that we're not.

Thinking there might be Communion after the service, our two boys went fasting to church, and so did Sonia, who came to the service not in her usual fur hat but in a woollen shawl.

Six children were baptized, one girl and five boys, their ages ranging from an eighteen-month-old boy to sixteen-year-old Mitya. They stood in a line, with the godparents behind them and the fathers and mothers last of all. They had to make the promise common to all Christians—that they repented of their sins, renounced evil and turned to Christ. Then each had to go forward a few steps to the font where they were baptized with water. Then, in a ceremony going back to the fourth century if not earlier, a priest touched their forehead, their lips, the backs of their hands. He gestured that they should roll up their trouser legs and touched their shins with oil. I could only suppose this was symbolic for the washing of their feet.

A symbolic lock of hair was snipped from their heads—the priest had some difficulty when he came to the toddler. They were each given a cross and a lighted candle, and in true Orthodox style there then followed a procession three times around the font, each child accompanied by their godparents, all of us holding lighted candles.

Having received Christ, the children were given a cross which they must always wear next to their skin. Then the priest anointed them with precious myrrh, a sign of being sealed by the Holy Spirit, and told them they were not to bathe for a week, so that the costly ointment would remain on their skin.

He recited the Lord's Prayer and the Creed, told them to come to church as soon as they could and receive Holy Communion, to communicate often, and if they were over the age of seven, to do so fasting. The priest then led them with their mothers to the *iconostasis* which divides the church from the sanctuary, where no woman may go. The boys were conducted in a solemn procession through the Royal Doors into the sanctuary, the priest carrying the toddler, while the only girl waited behind with the mothers until the boys came back, whereupon she was led to the Royal Doors, was given an explanation about the icon of Christ to the right of the Doors, of his mother to the left and allowed to kiss each in turn. My male chauvinist godsons hadn't realized this was happening, and they were hugely delighted when I told them afterwards.

So now our lives are eternally linked with a Red Army officer's family in the former Soviet Union.

Sonia's miniscule flat houses her husband Sasha and the two boys, Mitya (who's away now, having just followed his father's footsteps into the army) and ten-year-old Vladik. Polished furniture and floors gleam. There's never anything out of place. Each winter, carpets get carried out to the yard, shampooed in snow, the dirt thwacked out by carpet beaters like those my grandmother used to use.

Sonia brought her boys up in a communal flat in the centre of town, without hot water, sharing a toilet, a kitchen, with thirteen families. Privacy of sorts was provided by a curtain. The boys learnt to talk in whispers. Sonia refuses to speak of those days. She simply says, 'You can't imagine how hard it was. I know my house isn't a palace,' she adds, 'but it's a place of peace: a refuge.'

Her tiny kitchen has one power point for the kettle. Sonia has a twin-tub washing machine which she keeps in her bedroom; there's no room to use it. She does her washing in the bath, using a scrubbing-board. The fridge stands in the hall. Sonia, like everyone else, uses her balcony to store stuff. You see bags of produce hanging from balconies, as well as frozen washing. People even keep hens on the balcony. Cockcrow sounds across the housing blocks.

Sonia filled us with plump pancakes made with yeast, to which we added sour cream. Her husband said: 'I was brought up to believe in Marxism-Leninism and I got baptized last year. I can still hardly believe it,'—and once again we ached at the sense of psychological confusion so many people feel.

I was the first Westerner this family had ever met. Sonia invited me home for a cup of coffee at our very first meeting. I was standing at the door ready to leave when Sasha appeared, slim and broad-shouldered in his army uniform, resplendent in his officer's hat.

Trying to build bridges, I said in my very bad Russian, 'Of

course, Britain and the Soviet Union both fought against Hitler in the war.'

'Yes,' Sasha said, and his eyes filled with tears. 'I've only just found out. I've been reading Churchill's *History of the Second World War*. It's just been published here.'

Sonia herself told me that when she was thirteen the thought occurred to her, 'If it's as wonderful here as all our teachers say it is, why doesn't everyone want to come and live in the Soviet Union too?' But of course there was no one with whom she could share such a dangerous thought—certainly not her parents, who now feel shell-shocked by the sweeping away of a system in which they believed implicitly, nor anyone at school.

Sonia was a very able pupil and won a place to prestigious Moscow University, but chose Leningrad, closer to her home in an old Russian town deep in the forests to the east. Aged seventeen, Sonia lodged in a single room she shared with an elderly lady, a believer, who prayed before the icons in the corner of the room. Sonia's parents were not believers. As was the case with so many other people, her grandmother had taken her secretly to church and baptized her. She had seen icons in the home of an elderly aunt. Sonia specialized in old Russian literature and researched an unpublished sixteenth-century Christian text, and faith is flowering for her. It's really only since her husband's baptism that she has allowed herself to explore more deeply. But now she's eager to stand in front of the icons in our room and pray, telling the Lord about her concerns for the school and her family, eager to read the New Testament and the few Christian books we're able to get hold of.

Writers like C.S. Lewis enjoy great popularity here, and it was a red-letter day when I managed to get hold of a copy of Tolkien's *Lord of the Rings* in its new Russian translation and bring it home for Mitya. He has read it until the covers are almost falling off.

We left Sonia's at 10.30p.m. It took us about an hour to travel home on the bus and the Metro, with a change in the city centre. A tall building beside the bus stop had a thermometer showing the temperature—a balmy twenty-one degrees. The Metro was crowded. The up escalators were full of families carrying gladioli, chrysanths, big bundles. I guessed they were coming back home to the housing blocks after a day at the *dacha*, or out to Granny in the country, their allotments, or a friend's. These children with peaked faces would be tired for school the next day...

5

People—and Change

There's a meeting for all the teachers and parents connected with the school. Since Russian life works on the basis of 'who' rather than 'what' you know, we find, as we look round the room, that many people present are close friends, or relatives. A mother and son both teach in the school. More than one teacher present has grandchildren in the school. One or two even teach their own children, the children of close friends.

You could say it's like one big happy family. But family life is frequently fraught with difficulties and we feel a little uneasy at this close kinship group.

Boris introduces the teachers, including a new gym teacher.

'We are going to run in the park before lessons every morning,' she says, briskly. 'And we want the whole school to run together. Teachers too.'

'Yes,' adds Lena, Boris' wife, mother of five, and the director of the school, 'I shall run too. It's very good for our health.'

'What happens when winter comes?' A parent asks the question Stuart and I have been secretly pondering.

Of course we think the answer will be no more running.

But no.

'We shall run in the winter,' Maria Alexeevna, the gym teacher informs us. 'We are northerners. We have to get used to snow.'

So there's no help for it. Stuart and I are just finishing our mugs of tea next morning when we hear the shrill, excited voices of kids down in the yard. And even more shrilly—a whistle. Oh no!

We make our way down three flights of stairs. Stuart is wearing sporty-style pyjamas I tell him look a bit like a track suit. Both of us have a choice of footwear: winter boots, summer sandals, or street shoes. We have no trainers, not having foreseen that jogging would become part of our programme.

We line up in the yard. '*Zdrastvuyte*, comrade sportsmen,' barks the gym teacher in the style of the Young Pioneers, and the children chorus back, '*Zdrast-vuy-te!*'

Stuart joins in, grinning. 'Good for your phonetics,' he informs me cheerily. 'Listen to that nice round Russian "oo".'

There's more than phonetics being exercised this morning. My muscles scream as we jog round the park whose trees we see from the window. 'We run, we run, we run...' chants Maria Alexeevna, using one of those complex verbs of motion. Russian grammar in action. I shall never forget the word for 'to run around within a certain place'.

But how much more of this can I stand? Some of the kids are lagging a bit too. Luckily Maria Alexeevna gives us a bit of a break by leading us onto a football pitch where one or two men are swinging their hands down to their toes. We stop and do some exercises. Stuart stands beside five-year-old Pasha, who comes up to his hips. I stand at the back with the laggards. A few late-comers straggle up. I can neither hear nor understand the commands, and make only dilatory attempts at copying the stretching, bending bodies of the children.

'Do a head massage,' orders Maria Alexeevna, kneading her short black hair. 'Now—look up at the sun. We live in a northern climate. We need the sun. Stretch out your arms to the sun—feel its blessing... this is a kind of yoga, you know.'

Stuart glances back at me. Maria Alexeevna wears a baptismal cross, but few people who came rushing into the church in the religious fervour at the end of the eighties are well taught in their faith, and many are seriously into white witchcraft, as well as extrasensory intercession, praying over someone's photograph.

It starts to rain. I'm sure we'll go in—but no, this is Russia. One must endure, so we finish our PE—and return soaked.

Stuart and I collapse on the bed and swallow a foaming vitamin orange drink, but the children have to go straight to classes with nothing to drink, no showers or washing or change of clothes.

I'd like a shower too, but we still have no hot water. I have to heat water to wash myself and our clothes. The bathroom is still being shared by the French women. I do all sorts of physical contortions reaching up to spread things on the rope which holds the plastic shower curtain—only to discover it's placed so that wet washing drips on the floor and not into the bath. I decide I'd better leave a note to apologize to the French visitors. Stuart writes one in French, a language in which I can't put two words together, despite studying it to first-year university.

'What's "I had to"? *Il faut . . . Il me faut, mettre des choses ici, à fin qu'elles ne sèchent. J'espère qu'elles vous ne dérangent pas.*'

He looks at it with a puzzled frown. 'I feel it's not quite right, somehow.' I'm amazed he can write in French at all. This exercise in international relations has taken so long, the rain has stopped. I rig up a cat's cradle of string across our balcony, hang dripping washing there, and behold, a brand new twin-tub arrives.

Stuart left money for it last Easter. *I* really wanted an automatic washing machine, of course, but everyone assures us a twin-tub is much, much better. I can't really believe it, from my long experience of spending a couple of hours at a wash, soaking myself and the floor, as well as all the clothes.

There's great excitement as this machine gets installed and I try not to show my dismay at the thought that really all it will do is recycle soapy water from the spinner to the wash-tub. It will do that happily for hours on end. It will only spin clothes if there is water in the tub. It won't rinse—I have to do that in the bath. No wonder so many women here say they'd rather wash by hand.

I wouldn't though! How I miss my automatic machine! It was

my true friend. I sometimes gave its rusty top a pat of approval. I feel like giving the twin-tub a good kick!

After all the running and washing we're more than ready for lunch—discovering that today we have to take a roundabout route, picking our way through derelict rooms to a back door. Room after unused room opens up. I'm amazed when I see how big our building is. What potential there is here! But I realize sadly it would take an army of workers and millions of roubles to restore this building.

The reason we have to take this circuitous—and hazardous—route is that a sanitary inspection team came last week and ordered the canteen to be closed because there's no hot water in the kitchen. So it's officially not open and its outer door is locked. But folk are used to circumventing authority. The kids have to have dinners—and life goes on.

The only predictable thing is that nothing is predictable. Like the other day. I was supposed to teach one class and got asked to teach three with no time to prepare. At the end of the day, at five o'clock, I walked across the yard, my hands and throat dry with crumbly chalk. I lay on the bed, listening to the rustling poplars and the voices of children going home. I thought: what a miracle that all this has happened: that the Society got the use of this enormous building, that we're here sharing in their attempts to create a new lifestyle for the children of post-Soviet Russia.

Yet, as I was learning with the fifteen-year-olds in their Russian literature class, Russian attempts at democracy are no further forward than 1860, the days of Dostoyevsky and Turgenev. Voices which now shout each Easter, 'Christ has risen', not long ago proclaimed 'Lenin lived, Lenin lives, Lenin will live.'

I remember my very first visit to Moscow in the eighties—a bleak, frozen January day. Patient queues stretched as far as the eye could see. For what, I wondered? And learnt it was to see Lenin in his tomb. I thought then: at the heart of this mighty empire lies a corpse. And the contrast leapt to my mind—the Christian faith is centred on a Risen Lord, an empty tomb...

No one knew then how soon Lenin's mighty empire would crumble.

Nowadays Russians look at the dollar, inscribed with the words, 'In God we trust,' and say, 'Yes, no wonder it's so strong.' Dubious theology, but—money talks, and dollars are what everybody wants today.

We visit our friend Nadezhda, the art specialist who works in the Hermitage Museum amongst the treasures of the world and lives with her husband and their three growing daughters crowded into a tiny room ten floors up. She's been out of town all summer with the girls, but even so, life is hardly better for her. The *dachas*, we gather from her account, are as overcrowded as the housing blocks. There too she has only one room—in a barracks with forty families. And no water. Nadezhda has to carry buckets on a yoke from a well. This year the well dried up. She had to walk a kilometre each way with water. But she managed to grow marrows, and the cat enjoyed the holiday, the children tell us. Only he got used to freedom at the *dacha* and here they daren't let him out of their single room: their nasty neighbour once threw him bodily downstairs.

Fifteen-year-old Zhenya appeared—wearing too much lipstick. She doesn't study any more, her mother complains, and once she stayed out all night. She's like her father, sighs Nadezhda, with his wandering ways. But no wonder, when home is one cramped room with nowhere to study or relax, no privacy. The television is on the top of a wardrobe which bulges at the seams. Western films, adverts, come incongruously into this room with its piano, art books, icons. Zhenya's attention is riveted to an advert for make-up, to the gilded furniture in what appears to be a glittering Los Angeles drawing-room.

And there's ten-year-old Sima growing up in the middle of it, a slim, beautiful little girl, loving her blue budgie. She shuts the window as she coaxes him from the cage. And lively, naughty little Ania... She's so full of energy and fun, she's quite a contrast to our rather gloomy friend Nadezhda, and her solemn, intense husband.

We've known this family for years. I remember standing through a Palm Sunday service with Zhenya and Sima, tiny things of six and four, looking drawn with weariness, but patiently enduring the crowds, the length of the service. Zhenya used to play to us: Bach, Beethoven, Chopin, Mozart, her long hair tumbling down her back, and we felt we were in the drawing-room of a family sixty years ago. Only this was no drawing-room but their sole living space... and we've seen these circumstances break them. But Nadezhda still has faith. She refuses to complain, gives us a marrow she's grown herself, chutney she's made herself; says I look sad...

We both feel the awfulness of it and go home in pain. We wait fifteen minutes for a bus among the housing blocks. A man tinkers with a clapped-out milk lorry. It reminds me of a 1940s dinky toy—only 'dinky' (what a dated word) is what it isn't. The crowds at the metro too seem more shabby, down-at-heel, than ever. Stuart says, 'You long for the Lord to be walking in these soulless streets.'

We have a long metro ride home. A family with a child travel with us most of the way. I feel I should have got into conversation with them. But people have guarded their lips, talked in whispers even to their families, radios turned high, for so long and anonymity in the city is too strong.

I dream of my family all night.

Stuart is a man who loves people: people of every nation and language are his meat and drink. He genuinely loves all the details of their lives, who's related to whom. And not surprisingly, people freely share with him their sorrows and joys. So, instead of going to theatres, art galleries, even for walks, we visit people—even here, in a city renowned for its art galleries, its opera and ballet.

However, friends will phone suddenly and say: 'We've got tickets for this play, that opera.' Ballet tickets are harder to come by, because they are much sought after by foreign visitors. So we go to the theatre, though not necessarily to plays of our choice. I've sat through Arthur Miller plays in Russian, understanding not a word. We have been invited to slapstick, the two of us sitting mute and uncomfortably unmirthful, a small island of silence in the middle of the audience, while everyone else rolled in their seats, shaking with laughter. Humour is the hardest thing of all to translate, and that particular evening of hilarious comedy defeated even Stuart.

So we go out again, to meet another family, about to go to England for a holiday with their son and daughter-in-law who left in the seventies when it was a crime to do so. They were without any contact for years and couldn't even tell their closest friends what had happened to their son.

We go by metro to the newly-opened station, Dostoyevskaya. Instead of bearing the triumphant insignia of Soviet imperialism, the new station is decorated with grilles reminiscent, I suggest, of prison bars, to remind us of Dostoyevsky's time in Siberia.

Stuart stares at me in disbelief. 'Of course it's not Siberia: it's done like that to represent nineteenth-century St Petersburg.'

Oh well, we live and learn.

We come out opposite the Vladimirskaya Church, which Dostoyevsky loved. He could see its gold domes from the windows of his house. When I first saw this church in 1989, it was lying empty, its windows devoid of glass, its paintwork shabby, its five domes denuded of their crosses. It was one of the first churches to be given back. It's still very shabby, but it's one of the most popular St Petersburg churches, and certainly it's my favourite. I even like to look at its exterior, with the icon of the Mother of God, newly painted, restored to the wall facing the metro station opposite.

As we wait for a trolley-bus to take us to our friends, we watch a constant stream of people enter and leave the church. A banner is strung across a side road: Jesus Festival in the Biggest Ever Tent. Another placard proclaims in English and Cyrillic: The Great Volvo Cars Now Here...

The biggest tent. The best car. These slogans in foreign writing advertising big events offend Russians. Especially when Christ the Lord is touted in the market-place. Yesterday I saw an advert in English: 'Fast food'. Someone had chalked a bitter reply underneath: 'You eat the poison of the Russian nation.'

The trolley is crowded. We ride packed like sheep. The driver has a little tin cross on his dashboard. An old man whose white beard flows over his chest pontificates about the good old days, the changes. Women good-naturedly join in his talk—people just don't understand what's happening here.

Our friends welcome us warmly. We talk about being Jewish, having your race stamped on your passport; about pogroms in the seventies when their highly qualified relatives were dismissed from work. This was a motivating factor in the son's defection. 'We thought we were building a better world,' said Viktor bitterly—he'd fought in Germany, been a Party member. 'And all the time we were slaves...'

They have lived all their lives in a single room in this communal flat. Neighbours complained when the children practised their music.

They fear civil war, anti-Semitism. Only the other day, out gardening at their *dacha* they heard the sound of shooting. Their daughter Maria, an artist, had a roll of expensive, hard-to-come-by drawing paper stolen from her bag as she travelled back to town on the bus.

We eat fish soup, pancakes with boiled egg, a fruit jelly, fruit juice and preserves from their own berries and feel we are drinking in health for the winter months ahead.

But the weather gets hotter: a real Indian summer. I go shopping without success for something to kill the flies; see people laughing, talking; see a woman lying drunkenly asleep. Her feet are bare and filthy, one swathed in a bandage. I can't get hold of fly-papers, but I buy bananas—170 roubles a kilo (before long they would be 700, then 1,500). I walk back home, crossing the square dedicated to 'Leningrad—city of heroes'. My route lies along Old Nevsky Prospekt, an extension of the main street which runs right to Palace Square and the Tsar's Winter Palace. Old Nevsky was once a private street, belonging to the Lavra Church. The clergy charged tolls for the use of their road. I don't know if they kept the road in a better condition than it is now.

The buildings are grandiose and every one is built in a different style. Some seem reminiscent of Art Nouveau. All are very run down and used now as communal flats. There are shops along my route, but they appear insignificant, almost subterranean. Indeed, the entrance to many lies down one or two steps. I sometimes venture inside. The floors are dirty. People crowd round counters which seem to sell little except rotting fruit and jars of pickles.

There are more problems with shopping than the poor quality of the goods on offer. For a start, you have to remember to carry a bag with you, to take your apples, tomatoes, eggs home. And a jam jar if you want to buy some cream. Then you have to queue, not once but three times. You queue first at the counter, fighting to attract the attention of the assistant who is anything but that. (Soviet shop assistants do not assist; they seem to be paid not to sell the goods they guard!) When she's weighed or cut or simply slapped down on the counter whatever you've asked for, she scribbles the price on a scrap of paper which you take to the till. There you stand in a second queue and another unsmiling woman, who sits enthroned in her glass box with an antiquated till and a set of beads on rods, takes your money and gives you a receipt. You then take two pieces of paper back to the counter, press through the crowd—you have priority now because you've paid—pick up your goods and ease yourself thankfully away... To carry your bags home.

That's why I prefer to buy from sellers in the street, grannies in from the country holding out bunches of carrots, who weigh apples on hand-held scales.

This time, however, I get home to find that parcels from friends in Germany have arrived. They were sent nine months ago via a special aid programme. Great excitement as we unpack and share nuts, dried fruit, sugar, flour, chocolate, meat and tinned herring in sauce.

Church bells ring, startling the crows in the backyard. It's a festival, perhaps connected with the Feast of the Nativity of the Virgin.

We learn that Olga's youngest son, four-year-old Vanya, is in hospital. He had a bad asthma attack. I meet the two older girls and we go to see him and Olga in hospital. We stop to buy grapes from a booth on the way.

The children's hospital seems deserted. There's no sign of life: no cars parked outside, no one coming or going. Eventually we find two nurses in white overalls, sitting smoking in a cubby-hole place near a main door. They tell us to go outside again. And we are hailed delightedly by Vanya who is standing up at a window, with Olga behind him. The girls have brought food for their mother. There are no facilities even to make a cup of tea, no beds for the mothers to sleep in. We're not allowed in the ward. Our visit to this very sick boy takes place in a dingy area outside the ward—we sit on a row of four chairs. When we leave, Olga and Vanya walk to the front door with us. The corridor is heavy with the smell of stale smoke. There are doors marked head doctor, but no one about, no one at all.

Through all this the teaching, scheduled and unscheduled, continues. Stuart and I share Bible teaching with the fourteen to fifteen-year-olds in the tenth class, involving plenty of preparation in Russian which pirouettes on Stuart's tongue. Yet even he has difficulty understanding the quick, colloquial speech of the teenagers.

And English, English, English. Everyone wants English here, just as the nineteenth-century rich and genteel used to learn French. I wage a constant campaign for the preservation of the Russian language, not least when a group of poets called their journal— *daidzhest*—'digest'.

You see adverts: 'dansingkholl, intimn show'. One old Communist complains: 'I was married for forty-eight years and saw no woman's nakedness, except my wife's. Now look at the pornography, the naked women you see everywhere.'

'And you like to watch them on the telly, Granddad,' his family tease him.

But this old man is loyal: fifty-four years in the Party. He keeps a portrait of Lenin above his bed. This is no Judas, no Peter even, who says, 'I never knew him.' For him, Yeltsin is the Judas. 'He has betrayed our Constitution,' he complains.

There are others who think the same way. As winter looms ahead, with untold hardships for so many, as foreign goods appear in formerly empty stores, and Russians see foreign brand-names being sold at prices few can afford, I see the words 'Yeltsin-Judas,' chalked on a wall—and reflect that although few people know the Bible, here is a name which has remained in the consciousness of a nation, who now know the bitter taste of betrayal.

6

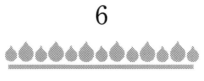

Aida

When we are asked, as we so often are, 'Why go to Russia?' we have to say that part of the answer is a person—Aida.

Aida's story would take not just a chapter, but a book. But first I have to flash back thirty years to the 1960s, when it was impossible for undergraduate language students to spend more than a few weeks at a summer school in the USSR. And no Soviet citizens got out unless they were totally trusted by the Party, or were well into middle age and left their next of kin at home.

The only opportunity to meet Russian people—even though students were supposed to be there to improve their language— was through officially arranged meetings. It was the same for Soviet students of Western languages—they could never meet a native speaker, far less study in the country whose language they were supposed to be mastering. Nor could they learn about its customs.

Over and over again I meet English language experts who tell me 'I adore England', who speak with heavy accents, repeat Russian idioms in English (a favourite is 'we welcome dear guests of our beloved homeland') and who know absolutely nothing about our way of life. Indeed Soviets were fed such totally false ideas about the UK that in my first months in St Petersburg I felt it was a privilege simply to be here and (I hope) reflect something of the truth.

One school textbook for young teenagers solemnly informs

the students that the four most important people in English history are: Robin Hood, William Shakespeare, Robert Burns (gulp!) and Henry Pollitt—who, I had to be informed, founded the British Communist Party!

There's a problem for Bible teachers too: interpreters go to pot over religious language. We've heard the *Apostle* Paul being called Pastor Paul; 'all we like *sheep* have gone astray' translated as 'all we like rams have gone astray'—and a few other howlers...

However, back to the sixties. So far apart were our worlds then, that once when I asked the International Operator if I could phone Leningrad, she said: 'Of course!' Then, less confidently, 'Where is Leningrad? Is it somewhere in Germany?'

All printed matter was carefully censored and letters were read, of course. One of my letters to Stuart arrived with coffee stains on the page. A little bit hard, since we were carrying on our courtship, and it was only too easy to imagine the censors' snickers.

At the very end of Stuart's first visit to Leningrad in 1961, when he went as an undergraduate language student on a summer course funded by the British Council, he had a free Sunday. He decided to go to church, but the problem was finding one which was open. There were only fifteen churches open for worship in the whole city.

So he went (a little naïvely) to the Tourist Bureau. The female clerk in the Tourist Information Centre sneered at the twenty-one year-old Scottish student. 'Church is for fools and old women,' she scoffed—and a man waiting at the counter agreed. They were reflecting the propaganda of the day. Everyone knew that religion was for obscurantists, not for progressive Soviet citizens.

However, they told him where he could find a Baptist church and after the service a slim girl called Aida, with thick shoulder-length hair, a large mouth and intense brown eyes came up to him with questions about the Christian faith.

It was difficult—and dangerous—to talk to foreigners. So Stuart asked what seemed to him an obvious question, 'Why don't you speak to your pastor?'

'I don't trust him,' Aida replied bluntly, 'and I trust some of the elders even less.'

That reply shook him. It seemed exaggerated, even slightly paranoid. But it was the truth, as Stuart was to learn for himself in 1963 during a hard, lonely year in Leningrad. The pastor used to send for Stuart to come into his vestry before the service.

'It is not necessary for you to stand through our service with other believers,' he would say, 'come and sit at the front with the elders.'

He wasn't thinking of the comfort of the young foreigner. He didn't want him to mix with the congregation; didn't want the congregation to pass on hard facts, for any sort of persecution of believers was officially denied.

On one occasion during that time in 1963 a young couple from the church invited Stuart to their flat—ostensibly for a party to celebrate the birth of their son, actually for a time for Christians to meet together (something strictly forbidden outside the walls of a registered building). Stuart, a sociable soul and starved of contact with Russian people, accepted gladly. But hardly had he arrived in the tiny half-room the young couple had in a communal flat, when his friend asked if he would put his coat on again and 'go for a walk'. Once they were out in the street, the young man asked if Stuart would leave. 'Someone's just tipped me off—the pastor's coming; it would be dangerous for us if he saw you here,' he explained. And Stuart understood, sadly, that there was a real danger the pastor would report the young family's friendship with a foreigner to the police. The Soviet law on religion stated that one might believe in God, that believers were free to 'practise their cult'—but only within the walls of an officially registered building. In fact, permission to register a congregation was often refused and, where it was given, the price was high: the leadership was slavishly in the hands of the State. Elders, and priests and pastors were frequently tools of the KGB—often, indeed, KGB agents—whose job was to inform on their own congregation.

It was against this background that Aida's meetings with Stuart took place.

Stuart's third letter to me in September 1963 reported guardedly: 'I have met our friend. She is one of us.'

So I understood that Aida had become a Christian.

Another letter, posted from Helsinki—he could relax his guard a little bit because the letter was being sent 'pigeon post', but still he wouldn't name her—said: 'A. came to my hostel today. This is dangerous as I know her visits to a foreigner are being noted...' (Aida had to leave her identity card downstairs in the porter's box and the person on duty would immediately inform the KGB, which is why the pastor in his turn tried to prevent Stuart from mixing with anyone other than those trusty henchmen, the elders.)

The letter continued: 'She brought me newspaper cuttings from the official press reporting how one Baptist prayer house had been bulldozed to make room for flats, another had been turned into a library: the caption here read: "Baptist prayer house serves Socialist minds." There was a picture of children with their hands clasped in prayer with the caption: "These children have now been taken from parents who taught them to do such vile things." '

Aida's great concern was to get this sort of information out to the West. She was sure that if people knew of this violation of the basic human right to worship God and to teach one's faith to one's children the whole story would be different.

In fact, the picture did not change for another twenty-four years, during which time there was steady campaigning by a few informed groups, most importantly in the UK by Keston College, a research and study centre then in Kent, now in Oxford.

The campaigning was one thing, but it was people like Aida who ran huge risks, struggling for belief to become a personal right in the Soviet Union.

Aida gave up her job, thereby losing her all-important *propiska*, that essential piece of paper which gives you the right to live in a certain place—and Leningrad was a much sought-after place. People even contracted paper marriages to come and live there.

But Aida, who a year before had stood on the main street, Nevsky Prospekt, on New Year's Eve handing out postcards urging her fellow countrymen to turn to God—a thing absolutely unheard of then—had already taken enormous risks. She was in serious trouble, and had already been brought before the Young Communist courts.

This was at a time when the Soviet conquest of space seemed assured. The first sputniks had circled the earth. Yuri Gagarin had flown into the cosmos—and returned with the confident boast: *'Boga nyet.* There is no God out there.' Religious people were ridiculed as never before and Aida was portrayed in the Soviet Press as a deluded idiot who had got herself caught up in some grandiose Baptist scheme for her own self-glory, and, worse, as traitor to the great Soviet dream.

Aida wrote a reply to these virulent attacks, but it was never published.

Early in 1964 Aida went to the Ukraine where renewal was, as she put it, 'spreading like forest fire'. She became friendly with Pastor Georgi Vins, who was to suffer for years in the Gulag before he was finally deported, with his daughter Natasha.

As Aida tried to get back to Leningrad she saw a fleet of police cars guarding the entrance to the railway station and knew they were waiting for her. Amazingly, a tourist bus pulled up and the police cars disappeared in a flash. Aida disappeared too. She jumped on a bus going in the opposite direction and made her way back to Leningrad unobserved, bringing Stuart stories of trials and arrests, begging him to take this information out of the country when he left at the end of May.

All this Stuart told me by 'pigeon post', some of it in letters he wrote from Poland, where he spent Easter of that year, some of it reported in the most general terms and posted from Helsinki or Stockholm through the kindness of other foreign students who agreed to mail the letters for him.

Pastor Vins and others refused to register their congregations, knowing that to do so would make them tools of the KGB. They were hounded and arrested on charges of being unemployed, a crime described as parasitism. Christian women like Aida formed the first human rights groups in the USSR, calling themselves the Council of Prisoners' Relatives. They attended trials, took full notes of the persecution endured by schoolchildren as well as by church leaders, and wrote appeals to the United Nations, to heads of State, even to the heads of the USSR, knowing that they were being earmarked themselves for more trouble.

Aida threw in her lot with the unregistered congregations who met in the forests secretly before daybreak, in thick snow in winter, eaten alive by mosquitoes in summer, and were were always at risk of being the subject of police attacks and dawn raids when police would drag women along the ground by their hair.

The leaders of these congregations were in constant danger. Ordinary members would be ridiculed, would never receive promotion at work, and might well be fined—though they all worked for a pittance. Their children would not be allowed to go on to higher education.

Aida put herself right in the line of fire by her desperate desire to plead on the world stage for justice for her people. Knowing too that very few believers possessed any religious literature, far less a Bible, Aida received copies of those forbidden books, New Testaments, and distributed them to fellow believers who came to her from congregations scattered across the breadth of Russia. This was highly dangerous: not even her closest friends knew what she was doing.

At one point, however, Aida was forced to leave a packet containing New Testaments in a left-luggage locker at the station where she had arranged to meet someone travelling specially to Leningrad in order to take them in his luggage to his church.

When she went back to collect her parcel the locker was empty. The precious books had been confiscated (a euphemism for stolen), and since she'd signed a receipt, it was obvious to whom the New Testaments belonged.

She was subjected to a fourteen-hour search. Precious copies of Christian books which she'd copied out by hand were taken from her, together with her Bible—and her freedom.

Stuart told me that friends in the registered church had warned Aida to be more careful. She knew what risks she ran—and paid the price.

By the time Stuart left Leningrad by sea at the end of June, 1964, Aida's 'home' was the floor of a railway waggon lived in by a very poor elderly Christian woman. Her job (she'd been a technician in a laboratory) was downgraded to a factory job, putting tops on bottles. Stuart left the country, often being subjected to a major three-hour search. Aida was arrested and imprisoned. She was twenty-four but (as Michael Bourdeaux, director of Keston College, wrote in *Faith on Trial*, a book on the problems of believers in the USSR) already 'mature in Christian suffering'.

Aida has served two prison sentences. Her time in prison has furrowed deep lines across her face, and she suffers ill health, but there's something eternally youthful about her. When our daughter met her not long ago she put her at ten years younger than her actual age. She lives simply, unobtrusively, but she remains a key figure in the life of her church—and has been tolerant enough to come with us to gatherings with the Orthodox, a very rare thing indeed. For over twenty years we had no contact with Aida, until we finally met her in 1986. But she remained an inspiration to us. Her second trial was well reported. Baptist women who attended the whole three-day trial did for Aida what she had done for others and wrote it all down, despite the fact that, as the judge herself said, 'I can see everything that's going on in the courtroom. It's not possible to write down what goes on at a trial: a few notes, maybe, not the whole thing.' They then laboriously copied it all out on pieces of cloth, which someone wrapped round him or herself to carry safely through Soviet customs.

That cloth is now in the archives of Keston College. I saw it before I met Aida for myself: fold after fold of material closely written in purple ink. It was translated by Xenia Howard-Johnston, now Xenia Dennan, and it became the main part of the book *Aida of Leningrad*. Interestingly, Xenia's Scottish forebears, the Bairds, were engineers in nineteenth-century St Petersburg. Their firm was connected with many of St Petersburg's architectural features, not least the cupola on St Isaac's Cathedral. They also built the four handsome life-size gilt lions which guard the bridge we cross every time we walk from Sadovaya Metro Station along the bank of Griboyedeva Canal on our way to visit Aida.

When the barriers came down at last, and we were able to come and live here ourselves, we made sure that we had in our luggage our copy of her story to give to Aida of Leningrad.

7

Army Training

Sonia has invited me to go with her this weekend to visit her son, my godson, seventeen-year-old Mitya, who has successfully passed school and army entrance exams, following in his father's footsteps as an army doctor in the Military Medical Academy in St Petersburg. Mitya's had a strenuous summer studying, and now he's been posted to a special training camp out of town.

(Unfortunately I was still in Edinburgh when Mitya was sworn in and so I couldn't attend the very splendid ceremony in which young recruits swear their oath of loyalty to the Russian Motherland and the army.)

Sonya and I meet at Baltic Station to catch the suburban train. It's Saturday afternoon. People with dogs, children and bundles flow around me on all sides. There's a high façade behind me, bounded by two walls, one plain, the other with doors leading from the metro, boards with timetables, news of departures and ticket booths. I'm standing in the middle of a narrow three-sided rectangle, the fourth side being the open platforms where trains await their moment of departure.

As I wait for Sonia, I try to imagine when the station might have been built, but I can't make up my mind. There's an elegance about it which makes me think it's pre-Revolutionary.

And indeed the station was built in 1857. The three-sided rectangle is, in fact, the shape of the Russian letter P (П). It was a Rolls Royce of a station, paid for and owned by a baron to carry the highest aristocracy from their sumptuous palaces in Petersburg to the outlying summer residences of Peterhof (hence the letter P, representing each terminus of the route) and on to the beautiful summer palace of the Tsar built by Rastrellil—the same architect who produced the Winter Palace—and also Charles Cameron, a Scottish architect whose name is associated with many buildings in St. Petersburg. The Catherine Palace, used only for the brief summer months, which the Empress Elizabeth (fifth of Peter the Great's twelve children), named for her mother, is a Baroque dream with its 300-metre-long blue and gilded façade; its glittering assembly room, whose gold and crystal is caught in walls of mirrors; its adjacent rooms all leading off from one another, lined with malachite, Wedgwood, and even amber.

In a bitter reversal of circumstance, Tsarskoe Selo—the Tsar's Seat—was the place of the five-month-long imprisonment of Nicholas II and his family, on their way to closer confinement in Yekaterinburg in the Urals, where they were executed.

The palace itself suffered a sad fate under the Nazis, who quartered their horses in its glittering rooms as the German front line moved closer and closer to besieged and starving Leningrad. It was left roofless and plundered. The amber was stripped piece by piece and stolen. It has never been recovered, but one of the first tasks of the Soviet government in 1945 was to begin to restore the Summer Palace to its former glory. It is a favourite summer haunt for the citizens of St Petersburg who catch the electric train there, though nowadays you leave from Vitebsk Station.

The great arc of glass which spans the facade of the Baltic Station, whose unwashed panes still give an impression of immensity, was designed to celebrate the great technological achievements of the Age of Steam: the click of wheels speeding across the gleaming steel ribbon of newly-laid tracks, the white curl of steam... The whole design was modelled on the architecture of the Italian Renaissance, on the music of Glinka, on the Gare de l'Est in Paris.

All so sadly down-at-heel now: the old aristocracy annihilated; the new 'aristocrats' being black marketeers.

Sonia emerges from the solid wooden swing doors which lead from the metro. She's carrying a heavy bag full of goodies for Mitya. I've got a treat for him too: bananas. They're available in the shops as well as on the private stalls, but at prices Russian families can't afford. I notice Sonia's wearing trousers—it's the first time I've seen her in such sporty clothes. Normally at school, or if she's entertaining us at home, she's in a formal dress or a blouse and skirt. When she's doing her housework she wears an old, carefully darned pair of leggings. Today she's in navy slacks, a striped blue and white top and a thin blue jacket.

We board the electric train, and jolt out of town, past ramshackle wooden huts which serve as *dachas*. But I can't concentrate on the flat countryside I glimpse through unwashed train windows—the poor allotments, the people gathering in their produce for the winter—because Sonia is giving me a Russian lesson. People sitting opposite on the rows of wooden seats look mildly surprised.

Is Sonia showing off a little—not herself or her language but me, the foreigner who's making such strenuous efforts to learn the language everyone around me speaks without difficulty?

So forty minutes pass and we get off and cross the railway lines. Throughout Eastern Europe people cross right over the railway tracks, not using bridges or underpasses. It's probably safe enough because trains go so slowly.

We climb up the embankment and set off along an empty road— where we get a wolf whistle from two men in a clapped-out car. We laugh and joke about our 'casual elegance'...

I tell Sonia how good it is to be in the fresh air, to see the countryside, walk among trees. Apart from a couple of days with her parents, she's spent all summer in the city. Like other part-timers, Sonia earns money only for the lessons she actually teaches at school and at university, and earns nothing during the holidays. So she's been coaching the children of friends. She starts to tell me about her favourite holiday place, away in the North Caucasas, a small town, a spa called Kislovodsk.

The name means 'sour waters'. She first went there when

Vladik was four and, like so many children in this damp northern city, suffered from bronchitis and asthma.

She took him south to take the waters and breathe in what is reputed to be the purest air in the former Soviet Union. Thereafter they went there for family holidays, taking advantage of Sasha's post to use the sanatorium run by the Red Army, where, says Sonia, she and her husband received what she called 'underwater massage'. I can't begin to imagine what this might be, but as we walk past more wooden houses, plus one or two newer ones of brick, we plan a trip there together.

This happy thought carries us up the hill and into the encampment, past a wire-netting fence and a small guard box with two young boys on duty. I keep quiet and Sonia asks them where Mitya's section might be just now. We learn that he's been kept late, unloading a lorry full of potatoes.

We stroll up the path with parkland to our left, with wooden tables and benches set among the yellowing birch trees, and wooden barrack huts where the boys sleep and study.

A group of naval cadets in black-and-gold uniforms run by at the double. 'It's like this all the time,' Sonia tells me. 'They have to do everything under orders.' But I make no reply. We've agreed that I should keep quiet whenever anyone comes within earshot. It's unusual, to say the least, for a Westerner to be in a Red Army training camp.

Mitya appears, grinning from ear to ear at the sight of us both. He's wearing khaki—the boys aren't allowed civilian clothes. We wander under the trees, sit down at one of the wooden tables, and Mitya lounges back and lets his mother fuss round him, unpacking the picnic bag, opening a large jar of milk she's carried all this way, feeding him with his portion of the family lunch—cooked chicken and potatoes. I'm sure she'll have gone without to give her menfolk a bigger share.

Mitya chews his way through the feast and eats three bananas at a sitting.

It's pleasant to be outside, but we're in shadow here under the trees, and the cold of mid-September seeps through. Courting couples stroll by, other young soldiers meet their mums and sit at other tables not far away. We keep our voices down. 'If anyone asks where Jenny's from,' Sonia warns Mitya, 'you must say, the Baltic republics.' That's what everyone thinks anyway, but I'm not too happy about the lie. 'Say "a northern country",' I suggest. We talk about Mitya. Life is tough and he's wilting a bit in his third month in this camp. He's not allowed to leave, and I realize it's no accident that he has no civilian clothes. Any recruit seen wandering outside the camp in army uniform would be in serious trouble—and only at the end of the month will the boys be issued with passes which permit them to travel free on public transport in uniform. Soldiers always travel in uniform. They used to be the future heroes of the Motherland, but now, to me, at any rate, they're an uncomfortable reminder of Soviet paranoia—a nation which felt itself to be at war for the peace of the world.

Mitya tells me about learning to shoot, and I say, 'I'm glad it's not at us in Britain.' He asks me about army life in Britain, whether there are Medical Academies like the one he's about to attend. I try to explain the little I know about the British Army, and let him tell me for the hundredth time how the medical training he'll receive will be far better than anything offered in the universities and how the Military Hospitals where he'll work will be far better equipped, with higher standards, than ordinary state ones. And, of course, he and Sonia assure me, the Military Hospitals aren't for soldiers only: they treat everyone.

I keep my doubts to myself.

Mitya's looking fit and suntanned after a summer helping on collective farms and roughing it here, doing gruelling training on what seems to be a very poor diet of badly cooked, rotten potatoes, cabbage and the inevitable buckwheat porridge (*kasha*).

When he's eaten his fill we warm up a little by walking through the trees, looking beyond the camp to the distant city, where tower blocks draggle along the skyline and a great pall of pollution hangs low over the hazy sky.

There's a smell of sewage from the settlement of houses in the valley below us. The air feels damp. We walk among slender, yellowing birches lit by pale golden rays of the sun in scrubland where this young man is walled up with boys from all over the former USSR, doing everything at the double, up at 6a.m. with a minute to get dressed, two minutes to wash. Lectures, army films, tough physical exercise, cross-country running, chores, bed. Celibate. Only no religion.

When it's time to go, out of sight of other uniformed cadets and their relatives, his mother makes the sign of the cross over him three times as we part. I suppose he should have taken off his army cap. He's a bit embarrassed but pleased.

He's cold at nights and he wants to go home.

Sonia and I walk back to the station and wait for the train. As we approach the city, lights are lit. It's 9p.m. A fiery sunset spreads across the September sky. We watch in awe from the electric train. The sky is shot through with vivid red, orange, purple: a great banner of pomp spread above the tower blocks and factory chimneys pumping their pollution into this sunset symphony.

Then the city swallows us up. We enter the metro system, and by the time I emerge the sky is dark.

Next day is so warm I sit on the balcony outside our inner room to write letters home. I'm still enjoying this balmy weather, after an almost sunless summer in Edinburgh, and I ignore the cracks which slice through the brickwork above and below my perch in the sun.

8

Orthodox Spirituality

Stuart and I snatch a rare moment together to go for a walk after supper, which we eat as usual in our room, heating up leftovers from lunch. Because the teachers are supposed to pay for their lunches, which the children eat free, I often ask the ladies in the kitchen if I may take mine upstairs. They always give me more soup, more rice or macaroni with or without meatballs, than I need and I pep this food up with a little tomato puree or some onions and share it with Sonia who has a heavy programme in the school and three days a week goes straight on to her classes at the university.

It has become our habit to pray together before the meal, standing in front of the icons in the room, both of us learning the Old Slavonic prayers.

And the leftovers from that meal Stuart and I eat in the evening, adding Western packets to the Russian cuisine.

So, duly refuelled, we head for the park where we still run in the mornings with the children. I have to say that I sometimes give it a miss, especially when I have a class at 9.30a.m., but even so we're the only two staff members who appear *virtually* every day.

We turn into Alexander Nevsky Square, which opens out at the end of our street, and head towards the park, past the usual open-air stalls of crafts and icons which are so highly priced that they are strictly for tourists; past the sufferers from cerebral palsy who are brought here each day to beg in their wheelchairs; past the old grannies with outstretched hands, who bless passers-by with the sign of the cross, and the weather-beaten men who puff on cheap cigarettes and swig bottles of beer as they lean on crutches of knotted wood, or perch on upturned crates...

Singing comes from loudspeakers to draw us into the Alexander Nevsky Lavra church—and we realize a special service is going on, for suddenly there's a procession of clergy all around the church led by the Patriarch of all Russia, Alexei, a silver-haired, blue-eyed Estonian. He blesses us too as he passes.

A little boy standing beside his granny tries repeatedly to make the sign of the cross, Orthodox style from right shoulder to left, together with a deep bow from the waist. I enjoy the look of pleasure on his face as he finally gets it right.

A young girl standing beside me is enveloped in a traditional floral scarf, a long prayer rope hanging loosely from her left hand. She is enveloped also in prayer of such intensity I feel as if she is at home among riches I know little of.

For we knew and understood little of the great spiritual treasures in Orthodoxy before we were privileged to be introduced to this tradition by our friends, especially Olga and Nadezhda.

We learnt only slowly how to keep the Lenten fast, to bow as we enter and leave the church, to stand at services, hands at our sides, for up to two and a half hours at a time. We had to learn not to shuffle, not to shift from one foot to the other—that immediately marked us out, for Russians, old and young, stand absolutely still, giving themselves to God, like the girl beside me, like the little boy so solemnly learning how to use his body as well as his mind and lips in prayer.

In Orthodoxy people use their bodies in worship and, like taking part in a slow, solemn dance, it's important to move in the correct way. People kiss the cross, the ground, the feet of Christ, each other three times, the hands of the priest, the saints on the icons...

The saints, the Lord, the apostles are looked on as friends in heaven by the Orthodox. When they go to church they visit their friends, honour them by the lighting of candles, ask for their prayers, just as we ask our friends on earth to pray for us.

Nadezhda, the art specialist, has helped us to understand the meaning of the icons: green, for example, is the colour of the Holy Spirit and also of youth, red is the colour of martyrdom, and so on. Christ is shown holding his hand in blessing—we had to be shown that the very position of his fingers spelt the letters of his Name. Icons served as 'the Bible of the illiterate', and for the last seventy years, when the Bible was forbidden, icons in battered churches have silently showed forth the age-old story of God's grace to his people.

This came home to me very clearly when a friend in Moscow told me how a Sunday school class in England had 'adopted' her family. The Sunday school children had drawn Christmas cards: Santa Claus, Christmas trees and Rudolph the red-nosed reindeer. My friend's two little pre-school daughters drew Easter cards: the women with their spices, the Easter angel, the risen Lord.

I find that some of the children I teach are familiar with Bible passages because they have seen them depicted on the icons or know the prayers, many of which, however formal, are earthed within Bible teaching.

Gradually we understood how a thousand years of Orthodoxy has sustained this people even through the atheism forcibly imposed on a nation known as Holy Russia. When Communists desecrated churches, they were careful to remove crosses from the top.

The story goes that in 988 King Vladimir of Rus wanted to worship God. He did what Russians are needing to do today— market research—and sent ambassadors to sample the forms of Christianity on offer: Western and Eastern. The ambassadors from Constantinople reported, 'Your Majesty, we thought we were in heaven with the Lord and his saints.' 'That's exactly where I want to be,' said Vladimir, and to this day everything in an Orthodox church is focused not earth but on heaven. The building itself, with five domes—the central gold dome representing Christ, the other four the evangelists—the icons, the music, the candles, the prayers are all 'windows into eternity'.

I recalled my first visit to Moscow in the early eighties. As we got swept along by rush-hour crowds, slithered over frozen pavements, I remember I said to Stuart, 'How hard to be handicapped here, lame, elderly.' The disabled had no place; indeed a young Orthodox girl in her twenties was even then in prison for campaigning for the rights of the handicapped.

Then we went into church—my first ever visit to a Russian Orthodox service. There was no sign of the building at first in the ill-lit street. A door opened. A crack of light spilled across the snow and I saw old women bundled in shawls and heavy coats, bowing, crossing themselves as they entered or left the building. We pushed the heavy door open and stood inside. The gold, the light of many, many candles, the singing took my breath away.

It was 6.30p.m. mid-week. The service was already well under way—and well attended, not only by the elderly. I realized that here was a reality not to be found in Communist Moscow, in the stolid crowds, the well-stocked bookshops whose titles represented only one ideology, one set of political doctrines. I understood why the Orthodox treasure their church and do not want to update it or change it in any way. I knew I had found Tolkien's Lothlorien, the land of healing where trees stay gold all winter. The place, too, where the elderly, the disabled, come into their own. There was a demon-possessed man present at the service, shouting, crying out in distressing agitation, quietened only by the anointing with oil.

The dead were present too. An old woman, her face in death as smooth as a child's, lay uncovered in her coffin, guarded by the saints who watched from the icons, by the prayers and singing which rose around her like incense...

The liturgy, sung in a much older form of Russian, is rooted in Scripture. The prayers are rich and beautiful. Russians use the verb 'to read' to denote the action of reciting prayers. But they don't use books. People know the prayers by heart—prayers like this one, which is said during Lent:

'As the Prodigal Son I come to you, merciful Lord.

'I have scattered the wealth you gave me, Father.

'Take pity on me, compassionate Saviour, cleanse me and clothe me again with the robe of your Kingdom.'

Or this prayer after meals:

'We thank you, Christ our God, that you have satisfied us with earthly blessings; do not deprive us of your heavenly Kingdom, but as you came among your disciples, O Saviour, bringing them peace, come to us and save us.'

Morning and evening prayers include a prayer to the Trinity, repeated three times:

'Holy God, Holy and Mighty, Holy Immortal, have mercy on us.'

And simplest, yet most profound, the prayer which unites Christians of all traditions—the Jesus Prayer:

'Lord Jesus Christ, Son of God, have mercy on me, a sinner.'

This is the prayer the girl beside me in church would have prayed on her rope. And the prayer rope itself, each knot a complicated manoeuvre, is made with prayer, just as an icon is painted only after prayer and preparation, and never for money.

9

The Ones Who Don't Fit In

I go shopping for apples and return to find Stuart grey about the gills, being besieged by Lybov, a Lutheran, who wants him to go to the Ukraine to run services there. Instead, Stuart endures an hour or so more of Lybov's talk, takes baking soda and disappears along the corridor as I see Lybov off. We then go on to a three-hour teachers' meeting. My head feels as though I've been machine-gunned by quick, unclear Russian. We have a late supper. I run a deep, deep (yellow-orange water) bath and sleep.

Like a fly buzzing to the honey-pot, Lybov reappears next day. This time he has with him a 'deserving case', a thin-faced young man of sixteen in the regulation trainers and denims. His name is Sasha and Lybov says he wants to study in a religious school in order to become a monk. It's obvious to us he's on the make, trying to take bites of an apple way above his reach. This wish to be a monk is in marked contrast to his ready response to chat up two girls who study here in the Institute. He asks them if you're allowed to listen to music and smoke. Does he think this is a monastery?

Lybov, who speaks easily and expansively, tells us about his own life as an orphan, in children's homes from the age of three. The orphanage was enormous, 1,500 children, he said, who attended their own school—didn't mix with other children. Summers were spent in Young Pioneers camps. Never ever on their own. Then life in hostels, the army...

Against this background he's trying to enter the church...

There's something just a touch too nice about him. He's trying just a bit too hard to please us. And there's something very brittle inside...

(Later we learnt the truth about him; the sickness in his psyche which made him attach himself to the gullible, the reason why no church would let him into its leadership, why he had never married, why he kept company with the young... Lybov was a pederast.)

Sasha is virtually illiterate. He joins the dozen or so fourteen to fifteen-year-olds who make up the tenth class. There are eleven classes in Russian schools and Sasha had been kept in Class 9 in his own school for three years. Many teenagers stop their education at the end of Class 8—at thirteen to fourteen—and go on to technical courses, and remain for ever at the bottom of the pile. Those who proceed to tertiary education complete the eleventh class and then move forward to a preparatory class before college. Higher education has to be paid for nowadays.

We notice with amusement that Sasha's a big hit with the girls. Our pupils are the children of the intelligentsia. One girl, a cool, very haughty blonde has read Oscar Wilde's *Dorian Gray* in English. Although I share her desk at the Russian literature lessons I attend, she barely deigns to look at me, and certainly never bothers to speak. A boy of fourteen speaks fluent American-English. Another deeply religious boy, who believes, as so many people do here in extrasensory healing and white magic, writes: 'To become a person in the full meaning of that word we have to educate children to become God-fearing people, loving and respecting him in all his strength and glory. Children should spend the first years of life in the country, with nature so as to learn to love, appreciate and understand it...'

There we go again: the mystical feeling the Russians have for nature. This is a country of mini-Thoreaus.

Here's a fourteen-year-old girl's deeply felt piece of work on creation:

'I was at the lakeside. The sun was shining and bright rays

fell on the water, the sand, the pine trees. The sky was blue. Everything was so peaceful and beautiful that the thought came to me how almighty is the One who created such loveliness. Even someone without faith, looking at such beauty, begins to realize that there is a God, because an ordinary person simply doesn't have enough strength to create such wonders: trees, birds, water. Only God could give such variety to nature. You look around and very soon you begin to see God beside you. And it seems then as if God is in every little ray of sunshine, in every drop of dew. GOD IS IN EVERYTHING...'

Unfortunately, nature has been so polluted all over the former USSR that a high proportion of children are born with deformities. We've been told only one child in ten is born healthy. It's a country too which is ageing and dying: the death rate outpaces the birth rate. The economic situation is so bleak that a mother of one of our pupils, talking to me about her married daughter said, 'I hope she doesn't have a child.' Not: I'm longing for my first grandchild...

But apart from human greed and the oppression of serfs by their owners, there's no hint of pollution in the beautiful descriptions of Russian countryside the tenth class are reading in Turgenev. It's all way beyond Sasha, whose jotter is covered with 'Phillips' and 'Sony' elaborately written in English. In the end he's asked to leave. There's all this talk about being open to the needs of society, but the school could find no place for an uncultivated outsider like him.

One day he came to our room to return money he'd borrowed. He told us that the night before a friend had been beaten up on the electric train, slashed to ribbons, murdered—for a few roubles he was taking home to his widowed mother. The electric trains are dangerous at night, Sasha affirmed, and I've heard others agree. He says he prays, goes to a Pentecostal church but can't understand what's going on. Someone else who feels himself a misfit, Dima, a young teacher of Greek and a colleague of Stuart's, calls round. Dima talks about his path to faith. He was baptized Orthodox but became increasingly unhappy, to the extent that he felt he would lose his faith if he stayed Orthodox. He became a Catholic and speaks rather bitterly about the Society, saying he's cold-shouldered by some of the ultra-Orthodox members of staff. (Had we but known it, this was a hint of major difficulties which would soon take over our lives.)

Dima tells us that last winter there were instances of scurvy and lice among orphan children. When he's not teaching Greek he works with Caritas, a charitable organization, distributing aid through the church.

And as we are talking about the need among the poor, three more food parcels arrive from our friends in Germany, wonderful provisions which vary our diet, provide us with vitamins and enable us to treat our friends. We give Dima a box to give out to the very poor via Caritas.

Meeting Sasha, hearing Dima and others talk, helps me understand the contrast between our school and the hard world outside. At teachers' meetings we hear time and time again how children arrive in our school shell-shocked after their experience of the blackboard jungle of normal school. Several pupils, writing about 'the happiest moment of my life' say: it was the day I started this school.

I ask Sonia about this—after all Mitya has gone through the system and ten-year-old Vladik seems to be thriving in it, coming home, eyes sparkling, saying 'I got top marks again today.'

'That's just it,' she explains. 'He's able to cope, to hold his own. But tender little flowers are crushed.'

Unconsciously echoing Sonia's words, a girl in the eighth class tells me that the children in the school she used to go to 'beat me and tormented me every single day. Once they said I had to bring them each three roubles or they would murder me... It was so wonderful when I came here. I'm blossoming like a little flower.'

Sonia reminds me that Mitya was unhappy at school and always felt himself an outsider.

There were, of course, special schools for the cream of the cream, the children of Party officials who live in a world apart, shop in special shops, have access to a life normal citizens are denied.

Yet still, despite the cruelty, inefficiency and harshness, life is shot through by that mystical entity, the Russian soul. No one is left to suffer if they have friends—and indeed, everything works here through friendship. Or contact. Backhanders. People are offended if you offer money. You return favours with favours. You offer gifts. And receive in return. If you admire something, it will be given to you! We have several things we inadvertantly acquired simply because we admired them.

On Stuart's birthday, eleven-year-old Andrey from the sixth class helped me carry books back up to the room, a true Russian male. He carefully rehearsed the words of 'Happy Birthday to You'. Just for something to say—and I should know better by this time—I admired a badge he was wearing of the Tsar's crown. He hesitated a moment, stripped it off and handed it to Stuart.

For the friendless, however, reality is very grim indeed.

Valera who works at joinery in our house promises to put up bookshelves for us. He's a gentle person, an eternal drop-out: hair that looks as if it needs a wash pulled back into a pony tail, a beard and very thick glasses concealing most of his none-too-clean face. He's always drowned in dust in our 'madhouse', where he bears the brunt of repairs, doing work which unfortunately often collapses as soon as he's put it together. Valera is an intellectual. As he discusses the shelves he enthuses over Brodsky, his favourite poet. 'Shelves? You'll have them! From floor to ceiling,' he assures us. 'You should put your dictionaries here'—he picks one up and points to non-existent shelving. He has it all worked out in his head, but when the shelves are in place they collapse as soon as we put a line of books across them.

He talks about his past, without any recriminations, except against himself. He'd been involved in administering funds for prisoners, and served a prison sentence himself. 'But I behaved badly,' he says. 'I repented.' In other words, recanted, signed things... but refused to give away the names of any of his friends who were connected with the fund.

While he was in prison his wife divorced him and Valera now shares a flat with an elderly lady who resents his presence—she'd hoped to have the flat to herself. He still sees his twelve-year-old daughter from time to time, says it's easier to be a father when you don't have to live with the child and bring her up. He also supports an elderly mother and a brother, on the pittance he gets for his joinery work.

I read in a weekly paper: 'A world gone crazy... Our life is so full of anxieties it sometimes seems as though we've gone off our heads—all of us, whole families, towns, the whole country. And perhaps it really is so.'

So where does hope lie? Perhaps in gentleness between people. Travelling on the overcrowded metro to Sonya's for a Russian lesson I notice a young woman with a girl of about ten. I see tenderness, big, melting eyes, too much scarlet lipstick—it's the current fashion. The girl gets up to give an older woman a seat. This is unusual. To Stuart's intense annoyance, having been trained since childhood to give up his seat, adults stand and children sit—otherwise they'd be squashed in the crush. The girl and the woman hold each other, laugh. Are they mother and daughter? Or sisters? Their pleasure in each other's company is pleasant to watch.

10

Preserves

We visit Olga. The scenes in the city centre remind me of old pictures of evacuees. A whole population adrift, carrying goods on their backs, dragging bulging sacks on ramshackle carts. But at weekends these autumn days the metro smells strongly of onions. People bring produce home from the country. Everyone makes their own preserves. Our friends bring us thick juice of crushed berries, raspberries, gooseberries, blackcurrants, all grown and bottled by themselves. We eat healthily—but there's a long winter ahead.

One thing we find hard to preserve is milk. It seems to turn sour almost at once. The secret is, we're told, to boil it, but I make scones to share with some of the young people we teach. They're mildly amazed that I'm able to bake. There's this feeling that Westerners live in palaces, don't get their hands dirty like Russians do. A few years ago one of our friends saw me bending to wipe the slush our snowy boots had bought into his Moscow flat. 'Do you know this work?' he asked, surprised.

I'm getting to know the new children. The eighth class, the thirteen-year-olds, has doubled in size since last year and now it numbers sixteen. Two of the new girls wear fashionable mini-skirts and keep applying bright lipstick; one of the others scrapes her hair back in a bun and wears clothes that remind me of pictures in books of children in the 1940s. She lives in a world of Orthodoxy, embroidering icons, plaiting prayer ropes and writing stories in which everyone invariably heads off to monasteries and gets tonsured. However, that doesn't stop her from falling in love with almost all the boys in the class! So the young people are gradually settling in and getting on with one another.

Education—which means English teaching—seems to have taken over our lives. I cross the yard at the end of the day with chalk under my fingernails. Mid-week, we have a quick plate of soup and go off together to an Institute which rents out rooms in a school and therefore can meet only when the school day finishes. It's been going for four years now, one of the earliest private Institutes of Higher Education, and its numbers have grown so much that the foreign language section meets separately from its religious and philosophical faculty. We've been asked—inevitably—to do English teaching.

Stuart will give a course on the history of Christianity in the UK and I'll do one on Christian poets, from the anonymous 'Dream of the Rood' to Hopkins and Muir.

We give an introductory lecture to a crowded top-floor classroom of terribly polite, terribly sophisticated students in their early twenties. As we leave at the end of the evening we reflect ruefully that, after similar evening classes in Britain, staff and students often head for a friendly local. There being no such thing here, we head for the metro and stop to buy a bottle of beer from a woman who's obviously been standing in the street for hours. She's a granny, she says, and is doing this to eke out her pension.

All this English teaching is bothering me a bit. What is it, after all, which really preserves? I wonder if I can give my lessons a Bible basis. I tell the kids: 'your parents want you to learn English and I want to help you, but the greatest gift of all is knowing the Lord.' I see thirteen-year-old Lidia nod. It's very clear from her serenity, reliability, cheerfulness that she has found the greatest treasure of all. When I ask the class to write about 'The happiest moment in my life', Lidia, the oldest of a family of five, writes in her clear, firm handwriting: 'The happiest moment in my life was when I was six. I began to understand that all happiness comes from belief in God.'

Yes, Lidia knows. What about the others? We work over the parable of the Treasure in the Field, which I call 'The Shortest Story in the World'. They seem to enjoy this different approach, which is encouraging.

My feeling that this is a good thing for me to do is confirmed that evening when we realize there's a guest along the corridor, and we get to know Sergei. Sergei is about thirty. He's come here from Riga in Latvia, where he was born and brought up, and is now seeing Latvian nationalism make life difficult for Russians. He's a history teacher by background but he felt a strong calling to teach the Bible. So that's what he does now, and he has brought with him a bulky manuscript—his own handbook to the Bible for schools—which he's hoping to have published. He heard about our Christian school and travelled here at his own expense.

Sergei talks about his path to faith from atheism. When he was a student he had to do a research paper about the Pentecostal movement in Latvia. From a starting-point of ridicule he slowly came to faith.

It wasn't easy, he said, for someone like himself, with no knowledge of God in his background, to come to belief. He told us feelingly how much searching and above all repentance it required.

Repentance. Yes, so many people we meet pay lip service to the idea that belief in God is possible. People wear crosses. Even avowed atheists now have a discreet icon in the corner of their bookcases and invite their friends for festival meals, like Pancake Sunday on the eve of Lent.

But real wholehearted commitment like Sergei's seems rare, and we are both delighted and challenged by our new neighbour's faith.

Sergei tells us that his father was angry with him for accepting baptism, and once, when things were going wrong, he cursed God. Immediately afterwards he was dramatically cut down by a stroke which has left him disabled—but the family took this as a sign of God's righteous anger. His father turned to God in penitence and was baptized.

'Yes, there is freedom, now,' says Sergei, 'but people have to learn that freedom also carries responsibility. Each believer should carry his yoke,' he concluded, and he has committed himself to teaching the most difficult and socially deprived children, taking them away to camp and trying to show them the love denied them by drunken, delinquent parents.

I envied him his freedom, and we were glad to be able to give him copies of the Gospels in simple Russian and other books as well.

We find that many of the visitors from abroad whom we discover on the way to the bathroom or the loo along our corridor, or who knock at our door for information, enrich our lives. But Sergei had found what truly preserves, and meeting him warmed our hearts as the first days of October brought cold winds and days of rain.

11

The Clocks Go Back

It's the first of October. We travel by metro to the middle of town to hold the first ever Russian language service of Morning Prayer in the Finnish Lutheran Church, St Mary's. People carry cats, saplings, supplies... The carriage fills: the endless round of broken, beaten people.

'Heavy faces,' Stuart observes.

'Built to withstand the cold,' I say.

'Don't you think it's the Finnic tribes who were here before...'

'You've got Finns on the brain,' I tell him. 'Anyhow, some people look very Southern.'

Sometimes you look at a face opposite you that could only have come with Genghis Khan. Tatar blood still mingles with the blood of the Vikings, the blood of the Cossacks, the Slavs of old Novgorod, the Finnic tribes of the North.

People think Stuart has come straight from one of the Baltic States.

The only thing they say about me is (gratifyingly enough) that they're surprised I have such grown-up children!

We press through the crowds, ride up the escalators and come out of the underground into rain which has spread enormous puddles across the pavements. I'm wearing dressy shoes and get wet toes as we walk down Nevsky Prospekt, past the sellers of ice-cream, gimmicky toys, and books—books of all kinds: art books in French, German, English, beautifully illustrated. Some sellers stretch sheets of polythene over their stalls to protect their books from the rain.

We pause on the bridge of Griboyedov Canal, dominated here by the Church of the Blood, whose Russian onion-style domes gleam resplendent in gold, blue, green criss-crossed with white. This marvellous church, looking for all the world like something out of the Arabian Nights, was built on the scene of a murder. Tsar Alexander II was assassinated here on 13 March 1881 by members of a terrorist group called the Will of the People. They wrote: 'A tsar should be a good shepherd. Alexander the tyrant cared only for the rich. He was a ravening wolf.' Ironically, this Tsar, who had supported the emancipation of serfs in 1861 as well as other social and political reforms, had that very day approved further reforms. But it was all too little: the peasants lived in miserable hovels and had very little real freedom. So the Tsar was blown up—and the name of blood was given to the magnificent church which commemorates his death. It's been closed since the Revolution and for as long as Stuart has known it (thirty years) it's been shrouded in wooden scaffolding—until this year, when the scaffolding was stripped away to reveal the newly-restored splendour. Stalin was planning to dynamite it, we've been told. The fuses were actually laid, and it would have shared the fate of many beautiful, historic buildings. But the outbreak of war saved the church because the army needed all the dynamite it could get and the fuses were taken up and never ignited.

Beautiful frescoes all around the exterior show scenes from the life of Christ. Citizens of Leningrad, out and about in the streets, would stop and look up and, it might be, learn something of the story of the Saviour.

In complete contrast—on the other side of the canal—are the stately colonnades of Kazan Cathedral, built in 1811 on the site of an earlier church which Catherine the Great felt was too modest a building to occupy such a prominent position, in the centre of what was then the Russian capital. So the present building was planned as a complete replica of that most important church of the

Catholic world, St Peter's in Rome. Perhaps this corner of the city centre, looking from Kazan Cathedral to the Church of the Blood, illustrates more exactly than anywhere else in St Petersburg the two-sided nature of Russia: East and West. The two-headed eagle of the Tsars, which is now appearing again on coats of arms and even on coins, faces both left and right: east and west.

Tragically, the Cathedral of the Kazan Mother of God was closed and used as a museum of atheism. I never visited it, but Stuart and others have told me how offensive they found the caricature of all the worst aspects of Christian history. The bloodshed of the Inquisition, the worst excesses of any and every kind of Christian fanaticism, were flaunted here as a warning against the errors of religion.

However, an amazing thing has happened: the crosses are being restored to the dome of the Cathedral. It has been re-dedicated to the Kazan Mother of God. Part of it is still used as a museum, but a museum of religion, and I have seen solemn open-air processions move with mounted police escorts up the emptied main street, icons moving in the thin northern sunshine, and sonorous bells calling to passers-by.

Opposite Kazan Cathedral, standing between it and the Church of the Blood is Dom Knigi—the House of Books. It now has some very attractive translations of Western women authors—the Norwegian Nobel Prize Winner Sigrid Unsett, Iris Murdoch, Mary Stewart—and, something quite new for Russia, women's romantic fiction.

Of special interest to Stuart and me is the dome at the top of the House of Books. It is almost identical to one on top of Forsyth's—now Top Shop—in Princes' Street, Edinburgh. Both were built by the same Scottish family—Singer. (Russians, however, tell me solemnly this was a German firm—so much for Scottish chauvinism!)

So it's nice to have this link with Edinburgh which we see every time we come to this central point of Nevsky Prospekt.

Today we're heading off towards the building which once served as the main Finnish Lutheran church for the whole area of

Ingria. It was taken over by the government and turned into a museum of natural history, whose collection of stuffed foxes and dog-eared posters of butterflies is called grandly: the House of Nature. The church is allowed the use of only two tiny rooms for office/vestry space and an upstairs lecture theatre for their services. English graffiti is scrawled over broken desks, and an enormous concrete bust of Lenin weighing 400 kilogrammes dominates the main window. During services this gets hidden behind the curtain—but the bulge of Lenin's head is still plainly visible and his nose sticks through.

On our way to the church we turn off Nevsky Prospekt and cross a square with the handsome building of the German Lutheran church—once a swimming-pool, but now given back for services. The reconsecration service, with representatives from the Lutheran Church, the Catholic Church, the Orthodox Church—and Stuart—took place with everyone standing around the edge of the emptied pool. A huge restoration job needs to be done.

And in an imaginative bid to raise funds the congregation and friends sell tiles from the swimming-pool stamped with the picture of St Peter's Church. The pastors who served the churches until they were swept away in the killing fields of the Gulag are still warmly remembered by elderly folk who, as children, witnessed the silencing of their youth leaders, lay and ordained, women and men. Pastor Kurt Muss especially won the love of the Russian-speaking members of St Peter's congregation, for he took the trouble to master the Russian language, in which he preached, they recall, with sincerity and conviction. They remember him, still in his early thirties, playing games—on trips outside the city in summer, in gatherings in people's homes in colder weather. They remember his confirmation classes when his fiancée Yelena played the harmonium. The couple were married in August 1929 (the year of Lenin's law which virtually suppressed religious life in the USSR) but they enjoyed only a few months together. Both were arrested in 1930. Yelena survived, but at a price. She divorced her husband, whose memory however still inspires the children he taught, the young people he prepared for confirmation.

Even without its pastor, the congregation of St Peter's struggled on until Christmas Eve 1937 when they arrived to find their church locked—and no one felt obliged to give any explanation for this totally unexpected closure.

St Mary's Finnish Lutheran Church stands just round the corner. It suffered a similar fate. Although it has officially been given back, the House of Nature has still not been moved, which is why we pray among stuffed foxes!

The Finnish language service is coming to an end in the dingy lecture hall in St Mary's Church, but there are people hanging around the corridor, or bustling about their business. One of these, an Ingrian deacon, greets Stuart—says he's seen him on television. This was an interview centred on the evangelistic campaign with its huge posters advertising a 'Big tent of big wonders'. It's causing consternation in the city, and Boris had generously included Stuart in the discussion. Now we discover it's already been broadcast!

We discover something else: we've arrived an hour too soon. They put the clocks back last night. 'Spring forward, fall back.' We learn that autumn has officially begun.

There's a good smell of coffee. The inevitable Finnish coffee maker is on the brew in the office. An elderly lady talks to me. She runs an old folks' home near the Finnish border which aims to give very elderly Ingrian people a rest from the stresses of living in communal flats. A visiting Finnish academic researching into the history of St Mary's Church joins us—she speaks English but no Russian. So now I am speaking Russian while Stuart makes gallant attempts at speaking Finnish. When the conversation inevitably goes into Finnish, I am silenced.

Eventually we get a group of people together and start the service. Stuart acts as precentor.

'Do you know this tune?'

'No, we don't, but we'll learn,' old ladies assure him.

The place fills up until about forty people, mainly elderly

women and a handful of little girls, are present. There are no hymn books, there's no music, and no one knows the long, rather complicated prayers, although one or two voices join in the Lord's Prayer.

At the end people shake hands. One shabbily dressed old lady presses some grubby rouble notes into my hand for the church.

This will be our routine on Sundays now. We make our way back through wet streets which are considerably more crowded than they were when we emerged from the metro—an hour earlier than we had intended—and arrive back home to discover that our life is being taken over by forty-five seventeen and eighteen-year-old Norwegian school children and their two teachers. They're sleeping on Dutch camp beds in the conference room in the right-hand wing of our building—with one toilet between them that gives up under the strain.

The three stalwart ladies in the kitchen don't give up, though. They're providing three cooked meals a day for forty-five young people and still with no hot water.

Stuart and I both get used as interpreters. Yes, me too! And so I get included on a visit to the Russian Museum with the Norwegian group. How wonderful it is to be a tourist for once and cruise along Nevsky Prospekt from a seat on our own private bus!

Nevsky Prospekt cuts across central St Petersburg, linking two churches. One is built entirely in the Western style, with a tall golden spire, unknown in Russia until then. Dedicated to the patron saint who gives the city his name—St Peter—and St Paul it is built within the walls of a fortress-prison. The other is totally Russian—the Alexander Nevsky Lavra, dedicated to the saint who, like Peter the Great, had driven back Swedish invaders.

It was on marshland won back from the invaders that Peter founded his capital, which people living here still affectionately call 'Pieter'—in the Dutch form of the name by which the monarch liked to be known. The long street we now ride along was dug out of the marshland and forest by Swedish prisoners of war, a gruelling task, and dangerous, because in winter wolves lurked among the trees. Peter's new city was built on the backs of slave labour—serfs and soldiers—and thousands died in the process.

Autumn has begun. The Indian Summer is over, but these first days of October are golden, cold but sunny, and the trees we see from the windows of the museum are a riot of colour.

These art galleries—the Hermitage and the Russian Museum—are my two favourite things about St Petersburg, and I was glad of the chance to go along with the group and have the services of an excellent guide, who explained that the main part of the museum was a palace, built in the early 1820s. We admire wonderful floors, chandeliers, rooms gleaming with white and gold.

Our guide explains that until the time of Peter the Great Russian paintings were all religious. Secularization began with the reforms introduced by Peter, despite earlier warnings by the Patriarch that no heretics—Catholics or others—should 'command or judge Orthodox Christians... nor introduce the wearing of foreign dress'.

Peter's aim was to make Russia a great European state. He built his city on islands. There was only one bridge and people had to travel by boat. All along harbour walls were baskets where people put the kopecks required for their fare—low-paid workers travelled free. Peter's ideal was Amsterdam, and, himself a master of fourteen professions (he could make his own shoes), he planned his city in a northern European style and brought in foreign experts—doctors, shipbuilders, draughtsmen and surveyors, architects, (notably the Italian, Trezzini) and a mathematician, Henry Farquharson, from Aberdeen, who went to Moscow to set up a Naval Academy, the first secular school in Russia.

Peter's table manners had shocked the noble ladies of Hannover; he had not even known what to do with a napkin. The gentry of London, too (he stayed in Deptford at the house of diarist John Evelyn), had been taken aback. So the Tsar published a book of table etiquette, instructing young Russians not to slurp like pigs, to use a toothpick and generally not to eat like peasants.

But Peter himself could live and eat simply, his own one-storey house, built in 1703, could never be called a palace, and is known by the diminutive *domik*, little house, while his Summer Palace (1714) is a pleasant, modest building which stands in the 'Summer park' beside an artificial harbour, created so that Peter could go straight down a staircase and board a boat. He enjoyed mixing with humble folk, and his death at the age of fifty-three came when he caught a cold after saving some soldiers from drowning.

Peter had his dark side too. He sentenced his own son to death. He delighted in the grotesque; delighted too in dentistry. It was said his courtiers went more in fear of the monarch's medical experiments than of his towering rages.

So the Museum guide rushed us through the rooms of icons and on to a portrait of Peter the Great. But some of the icons in the Russian Museum have been painted by the greatest of all icon painters, the fourteenth-century monk, Andrey Rublev. His two huge paintings of the apostles Peter and Paul leap across the centuries. And, although our guide claims that it was only with secularization that human psychology became of real interest to painters, I feel that the great icons, however stylised, show depth of character. The main interest of the icon painter, though, was the interior life of the soul, which gazes powerfully out of huge tranquil eyes as we hurry through to a room of portraits. There are paintings of schoolgirls, full of character and charm, pupils of the Smolny Institute, the first school for girls in Russia founded in the 1760s, the reign of Catherine the Great, who wanted to set up free education nationwide for boys and girls. There is a powerful statue of Catherine the Great who—non-Russian and a woman in a country in which still they say 'long hair—weak intellect'—became as great a ruler as Peter the Great, carrying on the work of the monarch whose true heir she felt herself to be.

For me the interest in the Russian Museum lies in the paintings of the nineteenth century: the vast canvases of landscapes; historical scenes, like the Last Days of Pompeii, in which the painter Bryullov portrays families and friends putting sheltering arms around one another as their city collapses about them. There is the enigma of a storm at sea: the Ninth Wave rises hugely above mariners clutching hold of wreckage. Will it drown them or will it be the lucky wave which will carry them to safety? The golden light in the tremendous sky lets us believe the outcome will be a happy one.

As much as the huge canvases, I like the scenes of family life, peasants at work, at home, the details of their dress, their marriages, their customs, their countryside, together with the lives of the citizens of St Petersburg, rich and poor.

Nineteenth-century artists portrayed scenes from the history of Russia too. There's Peter the Great censoring the son he later condemns to death; there are Repin's Volga Boatmen, pulling the barges along the vast river; Cossacks and clergy; richly attired princesses, wrapped in furs against the Russian snow. There is also a tender Raising of Jairus' daughter...

All this housed in spectacular galleries, with views from the window out to the city, mellow in its autumn light. It is overwhelming but, as we sit outside waiting for the group to gather, some of the Norwegian girls say, 'These wonderful museums and theatres, yet there's so much misery on the streets. Why don't they take some of the gold from their churches and use the money to build proper homes for the poor?' Part of me wants to agree with them. In fact, I think the reason I feel less than lyrical about St Petersburg—for all its fairy-tale palaces, the sweep of its main streets cut through with its canals—is the grinding hardship of everyone in the milling crowds, the miserable shops with shoddy goods, and, above all the appalling housing conditions. As much as this place being the seat of the Tsars and the nobility, the St Petersburg I know best is the city of Dostoyevsky's 'Poor People', those gentle souls conducting a tender love affair in the poverty of overcrowded communal flats.

So I understand when the girls return in tears from a visit to church on Sunday: beautiful singing, devotion, and yet the misery outside—beggars, the crippled, the elderly standing with outstretched hands...

Before they go to the church service the students listen respectfully to a forty-five minute lecture on Orthodoxy given by a serious, rather long-winded teacher. They are all doing their best to understand the Russian way; and they've come loaded with boxes of provisions which they give out to all and sundry: the ladies in the kitchen, the Russian young people who have befriended them and taken them to their homes. A boy shyly offers me a Russian Bible and the remainder of his roubles to give to anyone in need. His teacher tells me this boy has manhandled a whole suitcase of Bibles here.

Their teacher insists in taking us and some members of the Society out for a meal. We go to the five-star Astoria Hotel. Hitler earmarked this top hotel for his residence once he'd conquered Russia—but thanks to the bravery of the people of Leningrad, who starved through a siege that lasted 900 days, he didn't get that far.

The hotel rises splendidly from smooth pavements in the expansive square close to St Isaac's Cathedral, which, like Kazan Cathedral, was used as a museum. Children used to be taken on tours of icons which told the story of Christ's sufferings, even though the voice of the church was silenced. Like Kazan Cathedral, St Isaac's has been reconsecrated as a church and its crosses have been restored.

It stands close to the building which, more than anything else, symbolizes St Petersburg: the Admiralty, begun in 1704, built in the shape of a letter P, with the River Neva itself forming part of the monarch's initial. Ship-building was carried on here and three roads lead from it, like the three prongs of the sea-god Neptune's trident. So that here, opposite the town government headquarters, now showing the Russian tricolour, we look back at the building which symbolizes it all, for the soaring spire on the Admiralty, like the Peter-Paul fortress, could only belong to the West. But Russia requires domes of gold and so the gilded spire gleams. Both the Cathedral and the Astoria Hotel stand at the end of what is said to be the broadest bridge in Europe.

Unfortunately, the service in this top hotel was very poor and prices, in currency, were high.

'Eating out used to be a favourite Russian pastime but we don't frequent restaurants nowadays,' someone said afterwards as we waited for a trolleybus to carry us home the five-kilometre length of Nevsky Prospekt. 'Waiters cheat. If they don't cheat on prices, they cheat on the quality of the food they offer.'

We felt bad that the Norwegian teachers had been given such an expensive deal, but we all made the best of our meal out.

So the autumn days go by: language study, teaching, being entertained—and entertaining the world.

12

What's In A Name?

Birthdays get noted, anniversaries and parties. The whole world loves a party, but surely nowhere more than here. Presents and flowers are ceremoniously presented, little speeches are made and everyone wears their best clothes.

So it's a major event when St Catherine's Roman Catholic Church on Nevsky Prospekt holds its reconsecration. This is the church I found closed only last month. Now it's been given back, although at the moment only one small room, which will eventually be a chapel, is usable. On our way to the Lutheran service we call by to give the priest, an old friend of ours, a card of congratulations. The atmosphere is so festive I decide to stay for Mass.

The tiny chapel, bright with new white paint, is already overcrowded. The crush is going to be tremendous. 'Please move further back,' a priest keeps begging from the front. 'Please, dear friends, once more I ask: move further back.'

The title 'dear friends' has a particularly endearing sound in a country where people call each other either 'comrade' or 'young man', 'young girl'. Or, 'woman'. Or 'Granny'. 'Sir' and 'madam' have long since disappeared. 'Ladies and gentlemen' is being used again now by TV presenters—even, sometimes, at public meetings, especially if the chairman (and it always is a man, in my experience) is an ex-comrade. However, in a country where people traditionally address one another by their full Christian name and patronymic (your father's name with *ovich*, if a man, or *ovna* or *evna* added), 'ladies and gentlemen' sounds both foreign and formal. 'Dear friends' is a happy compromise.

Many people tell us they are not sure how to address us. 'Stuart' sounds like a surname, so it's all right if they're speaking in a formal context. His father's name was Neil and 'Nilovich' has quite a good ring to Russian ears. But 'Jenny' sounds like the Russian diminutive for Eugenia/Yevgenia. So it seems too informal. And my father's name was William, a very difficult name for Russians to pronounce. It's particularly awkward for children in school, who from class one address their teachers by Christian name and patronymic—whereas I am just Jenny.

As for us, we get hopelessly lost with patronymics. It's hard enough for me to try to remember Christian names. Stuart has his problems too: there really isn't a wide choice of women's names: Natalia/Natasha; Tatiana/Tanya, Galina/Galya, Olga, Nadezhda/ Nadia...

Someone phones and says 'Olga here'. And Stuart will think it's 'our' Olga, only to discover it's Olga Vladimirevna, or Olga Alexeevna, or Olga Nikolayevna... It all adds interest to life, I suppose. Perhaps it would simplify things if we were all like the man in the Mass this morning. Here I am, wedged in now, pressed against the row of seats in front of the choir, who are busy warming up. The knee of an elderly person sitting behind me digs into me. I shift, and a girl's hair tickles my nose. The small balcony behind me is already packed to overflowing. And now a big man pushes through the crowd towards the balcony. His umbrella hits people. 'I'm here,' he announces in English to the world at large.

'I'm here' or 'it's me'... isn't that what we really mean when we give our name? 'Look, world, notice me.'

But here in the crowd there's a feeling of being at one with each other, even though we're strangers. So it's not so important to say, 'it's me', because every one of us has our place and we're part of this bigger thing which is happening all around us today.

The choir behind me gives a great burst of song, and now the clergy enter. At least, I guess that's what's happening because all I can see is the heads of the people all about me. But that doesn't matter, either.

Father Eugene speaks in his lovely clear Russian which I've always been able to catch the gist of, even in the days when I spoke virtually no Russian at all. I recall eating Easter cake once in his flat, picture his room, lined with books, icons and crosses—a tiny room which was the centre for underground Catholic services for many years.

The Catholic church here managed to survive even after the Revolution, I gather, in a church off the Square of the Uprising which had always been used by French people—or people of French descent—in St Petersburg. But in 1940, when France fell and the Vichy government took over, the priest in St Petersburg was told to get out, and the official Catholic presence all but disappeared.

I'm not sure how the French managed to hang on in the twenties and thirties. Swedish and German Lutherans were driven out along with the Anglicans, whose empty chapel with beautiful nineteenth-century mosaics—a style which might have seemed dated but is now almost becoming fashionable once more—stands beside the Neva on what was once called 'English Embankment' and is now labelled 'The Embankment of the Red Fleet'. The chapel, dedicated to St Mary, has a historic organ, said to be one of the very best in Europe. It is full of rows of empty booths belonging to the Soviet Tourist Bureau, which is running out of business nowadays because there is no Soviet Union, Russians can't afford to go on holiday, and the previous tourist spots—the Crimea, the Caucasus—are no longer felt to be safe. Father Eugene himself once held lectures in the chapel.

I know what a great occasion this is for him. 'Christ has returned to us,' he says. 'We chased him away. Now we must build a community for him, a community open to everyone.'

In fact, the note of this service is ecumenical. With Swedish, German and Finnish Lutheran churches in the neighbourhood, and two main Orthodox churches close by, the hope is that

St Catherine's, standing right in the centre of Nevsky Prospekt, can become an open place of prayer, as the text over its door suggests. The Archbishop reminds us, in fluent Russian: 'My house shall be called a house of prayer.'

He recalls the history of this building: generals and princes were buried here but, once the Revolution came, the clergy were arrested and condemned to death: 'The building was closed. A new creed was propagated, trying to build paradise on earth: a paradise without God.'

But the Archbishop's key-note is resurrection. 'Christ lay in the grave for three days,' he says. 'Christianity was suppressed for three generations... We think of unknown, untold suffering, arrests, imprisonments, deaths, searches, a faith sent underground...'

The Archbishop comes from Gniezno, an old cathedral city in Poland, but I only learn this afterwards and have to guess from his accent that he's Polish.

He recalls his time as a student in Leningrad, over thirty years ago. How sadly he looked up at the Latin text above the desecrated church. 'I've reconsecrated many churches but this is the highlight of my episcopal life,' he assures us, with emotion.

The choir sings full voice and so the service continues on a note of joy and celebration which does not waver, for two hours or more.

The ceremony is being filmed. But film won't capture the feeling of joy.

When it's all over, it takes a long time for the church to empty. I look at my watch. I've been standing now for almost four hours.

When I get outside I realize it's raining. Puddles stretch across the uneven yard. Some of Mother Teresa's nuns with raincoats over their saris are standing in the mud and rain outside.

I join the crowds in the street: the artists who draw charcoal portraits; the sellers of puppies and kittens, of a single pair of boots, of cigarettes and vodka, of china and glass; the beggars; the jazz musicians; the young boys in denim and leather playing heavy rock whose sounds echo along the underpass as I join the crowded metro.

In their different ways they are all saying: 'I'm here, notice me, help me, join me...'

I get swept on to the train by the crowds behind me. I'm standing sqashed beside some Salvation Army officers, two women, with a group of girls of about thirteen. Here in this militaristic city among so many soldiers in uniform, the Salvation Army is met with a kind of incredulous amusement. 'Army of Salvation', the hatbands proclaim in Russian. In their own way they seem as outlandish as Mother Teresa's nuns, whose saris draggle through the northern mud. But, like the nuns, they are already winning respect for the good work they do. 'We meet at eleven o'clock on Sunday mornings,' a helper tells me. 'Do come.'

13

A Visit to the Military Academy

The weight of the Red Army presses heavily upon me for a whole seven minutes today as a bulky officer is crushed up against me. I'm travelling in a crowded carriage on the metro to go to Sonia's.

She gives me lunch: cabbage soup, black bread with *tvorog*, topped with a scattering of sugar and thin sour cream. *Tvorog* is a cross between cottage cheese and Scottish crowdie. There are two varieties. The one I prefer is slightly sweeter. Stuart says, 'It's too cloying.' The sweeter version, which is much harder to find in the shops or market, is used to make cheesecake and that lovely rich white mound of calorific cream, *tvorog*, eggs, lemon, sugar, raisins which is eaten with the special, slightly crumbly Easter cake, *kulich*—and tastes all the richer and more gorgeous after a lean Lent in which dairy products and eggs are not allowed.

Vladik shows me his school books. I read his careful ten-year-old handwriting: 'The Great Patriotic War began in 1941. My grandfather was a partisan...'

In those dark days Finland watched Soviet troops march into their country: endless columns of tanks, machine guns.

Yuri Ivanovich, Sonia's father, was badly wounded as he crossed Karelia on skis. Yuri Ivanovich has told me how, as a boy of seventeen, he carried packs heavier than himself. He describes what it was like to be bombed by low-flying planes in the Winter War against Finland. The Finns wore white. The Soviet soldiers had no camouflage and showed up clearly against the endless snow as low-flying planes droned overhead, dropping bombs and spattering machine-gun fire. He said he'd lie in the snow, hands cradling his head and just hope it wouldn't be him that got shot to bits. Once, he said, the Finns caught an army nurse and tied her to a mine, so that when the Soviets came to set her free they would be blown up. The Finns, for their part, with a long and tragic history of being invaded by mightier powers, had seen the Soviet force entering their land: tanks, military might stretching back as far as the eye could see...

That's war...

After lunch Sonia corrects work I've prepared in Russian and then we go off to meet Mitya in the Military Academy. No buses come, so we go by taxi. The driver talks about his worries—what will happen next month when the price of petrol goes up? He's playing tango music and asks us if we ever go dancing. 'Oh,' says Sonia, 'when I was a student—we used to meet in someone's room, roll back the rug, put on a record and get up and dance.'

Which is how she met Sasha. He's a fine musician and was playing his guitar and singing the romantic ballads Russians still like so much. Sonia has a good singing voice too. Mitya has an amazing bass with which he serenades us when there are family celebrations.

I keep very quiet in the taxi. Taxi drivers charge high prices if they are carrying foreigners.

The Military Academy is near Finland Station. It's a vast concourse of buildings, some quite historic. It still lives up to its reputation as being the best and most prestigious military school in all Russia. The brilliant young poet Lermontov studied here in the early 1830s. Lermontov's forebears came to Russia from Scotland, and he prided himself on being able to trace his line right back to Macbeth, claiming that his ancestor was loyal to Malcolm, son of Ďuncan, the murdered true king. Also that the blood of the bards of Scotland ran in his veins, for he felt that his ancestry included True Thomas the Rhymer, who kissed the lips of the Queen of Elfland and in return was given a tongue that could never lie. Lermontov himself came to the Academy from a circle of adoring ladies and he found life hard—marches, parades, getting up every day to the beat of a drum.

Dostoyevsky studied here too, graduating in 1841.

Sonia shows me a big building in the shape of an English W dedicated to Scotsman James Wylie, who escaped the death penalty in Scotland to become doctor to the Tsar himself. Wylie graduated from Edinburgh University faculty of medicine and also had a diploma from the University of Aberdeen. He came to Russia in 1790, at the age of thirty-two. He has the distinction of organizing the first independent military medical schools in Russia and founded a military medical journal, which is still published today. Wylie was anxious to improve the standards of hygiene for soldiers on the battlefield, who were especially prone to diseases like cholera and typhoid. He died at the age of eighty-six and is buried in St Petersburg.

Sonia shows me the handsome statue put up after Wylie's death, dedicated to Yakob Vasilevich Villiye. It's in a small park, bright with autumn leaves, and is a quite notable piece of sculpture: a life-sized statue of Dr Wylie, surrounded by scenes from military life and displaying the two-headed eagle of the Tsars.

So Scotsmen too have played their part in the Russian Army, and I'm glad Sonia showed me this fine piece of sculpure and the hospital shaped like a W.

We go on to meet Mitya. He's still suntanned, but he's tired and stressed. His boss keeps putting him on guard duty. He has to stand on duty for two or three hours, day or night, and he's worried about falling behind in his studies. The students live in overcrowded conditions in dormitories of ten all opening off a long corridor, with no privacy to study, inadequate places to have a wash. Life is controlled, not by a drum, as in Lermontov's day, but by a whistle, from getting-up time till lights out.

We sit on a park bench and Sonia unpacks a picnic—once again I've added bananas. A mangy cat heads across, hoping for food. Sonia blesses Mitya, drawing him discreetly away from passers-by.

We walk past the whole complex of military buildings—some small palaces, some large old buildings, dedicated now to Soviet heroes. Some offer the teaching of foreign languages. I ask whether ordinary citizens can come here. Sonia indicates that the hospitals are for soldiers from all over the former Soviet Union, for their families, and also for cases which ordinary hospitals aren't able to treat.

We walk to the banks of the Neva, and look across to the university buildings. It's good to see the expanse of sky and water, glowing in the evening light, whose colours ripple across the oily waters of the Neva.

Perhaps it was on a night like this that the sunset sky inspired the young Dostoyevsky to see in the clouds of mist swirling over the river that St Petersburg of communal flats he wrote of in *Poor People*—where the poor office clerk Makar Devushkin hoarded his candle-ends in order to write, late into the night, tender letters to his beloved 'little dovey' Barbara, whose face he sometimes has the joy of glimpsing at the window across the courtyard. Devushkin describes life in St Petersburg in terms which seem not so unlike life in communal flats today:

'They live here, one to a room, two, three... Don't ask about order... Of course, some people are all right, educated... We have a big kitchen, spacious, light. It does smell a bit in the mornings when people are frying fish, yes and it's damp, water runs everywhere, but it's paradise in the evening. In our kitchen there's always laundry hanging to dry, and my room's just off the kitchen, so the smell annoys me a bit, but it's all right, you get used to it...'

...just as people today have to put up with drunk neighbours, with other people's pop music, cooking smells, a toilet someone else has just used, a bath someone else is using just now...

The sun is setting behind the tall golden spire of the Peter-Paul fortress, in whose dreadful dungeons Engineer Lieutenant Dostoyevsky, already epileptic and turning to prayer to help him through the giddiness and hallucinations which preceded his seizures, was imprisoned. His crime? Radical ideas. He supported an ending of strict censorship and had read a letter at a literary gathering which criticized the Orthodoxy which Dostoyevsky was later to endorse so wholeheartedly.

The walls of these gloomy dungeons are thick, and even now penetratingly chill. Some of the brightest and best minds and hearts of Russia have languished here, many never to emerge from the unlit dungeons. When Dostoyevsky was incarcerated the walls were covered in mould and the damp penetrated to every fibre of the prisoner's bones. He was allowed no writing materials, no books, no candle, no tea.

Dostoyevsky left this grim fortress on 22 December 1849—to be led out with his fellow-revolutionaries to Semyonovsky Square, a large parade ground. Here he kissed the cross, was tied to a stake and blindfolded, awaiting the shots which, he devoutly believed, would carry him to Christ.

It was a cruel trick. Tsar Nicholas I wanted no martyrs and had already decided that the fate of these prisoners would be not death but a ten-pound chain about their legs, and Siberia. They could not know this, however, as they stood at the stake, shivering in their fresh linen shirts, awaiting death.

And then, at the last minute—a reprieve. The blindfolds were removed. The prisoners saw again St Petersburg's golden spires, the clear December sky. So great had been the tension, so prolonged the eight-month suffering in the dungeons of the Peter-Paul fortress, so enormous the relief, that one of the reprieved prisoners went mad. Dostoyevsky himself never forgot that moment. He refers to it again and again in his writings. Ahead lay an appalling journey, ten years of grinding labour, during which time he was always in chains and felt, as he put it, as though he had been buried alive and interred in a coffin. But in those moments on the St Peterburg parade ground, Dostoyevsky felt like a man new-born. His greatest novels still lay ahead of him.

Now, in the St Petersburg which featured in *Crime and Punishment* and so much of Dostoyevsky's work, I watch two men fishing from the bridge. I wonder if fish from such polluted waters are safe to eat.

Sonia and I talk as we walk beneath the sunset sky. I ask her how she views all the changes from the mid-eighties on. She says, 'Of course, it was wonderful.' Wonderful to receive news, real news about the world outside which had been shut off for so long. Wonderful to see churches opened—the time when everyone celebrated the Thousand Years of Christianity in Russia and the church suddenly became public, acceptable... But now people are afraid and suffering financial hardships. For example, explains Sonia, they used to go out as a family to the Tsars' summer palace out of town, to Pavlovsk and the palace of Peter the Great. Now fares are too expensive. Or they would go to the cinema together. Last Sunday the boys went to the cinema alone: they couldn't afford for the whole family to go. Mitya bought Vladik an ice-cream, but didn't have one himself.

Freedom has brought quick riches for some, hardship for most ordinary families. It has brought everyone fear, for law and order are visibly breaking down and no one feels safe now out and about in the streets.

We stand at a tram stop. A container lorry from Hamburg is parked opposite. The sight of this foreign vehicle leads Sonia to mention that Solzhenitsyn has predicted that the mafia will rule Russia not for seventy years, but for one hundred and seventy...

One of the triple-car St Petersburg trams rattles along and we board. We go to the metro station Gor'kovskaya, following the route Stuart and I took a year ago as we attended a memorial ceremony for the victims of Stalinism (it's still put that way, exonerating Lenin). We found ourselves that day joined by more and more people, all with personal experiences of the Siberia Dostoyevsky knew in his time, and we gathered around a mass grave, lit candles and stood in silence as each person buried there was remembered, as people recalled their own sufferings and asked for redress.

Sonia and I part at the metro and travel home our separate ways.

THE FIRST SNOW

14

A Hint of Chill

It's now the middle of October. Leaves still cling to the trees in our yard but the first snow starts to swirl down in blizzards. We've been back six weeks now and we've still had no letters from any of our family, nor has the container arrived with essential luggage (including winter coats) which we sent by sea.

Lidia Vasilevna, a member of the Society and mother of one of the children in the school, talks about her path to faith. She says that for Russians faith can only come through tragedy, explaining that she lost her grandparents in the siege of Leningrad and against that background her mother had had her baptized, although there was no other Christian input in her early life. A physicist, she started going to church when she was in her twenties, secretly, she said, wearing a scarf pulled low over her head. She joined the Society because she feels it's offering hope for Russia today.

We're grateful to Lidia in the following days. A phone call comes saying the ship with our things on board will be arriving on Monday.

Sounds easy: you go to the docks, and pick up the stuff. But nothing is that easy here.

Stuart gives up an entire week of his life to find out, first, which dock the ship is due in at, and second, whether it has unloaded. Then, most importantly, he has to find the right official with the right piece of paper who can authorize him to take our own possessions from the dock. And of course they have to be subject to Customs control, requiring more delay, more officials, more essential pieces of paper.

Lidia's moral support here is invaluable. She goes three times to the docks with Stuart—each time they're away for five or six hours. She makes phone calls and we smile across our table at each other as we hear this very gentle lady harangue officials on Stuart's behalf. 'It's too much for an elderly man,' she says.

'It's all right,' other friends reassure Stuart when he jokes about this new description he's been given. 'Lidia was just trying to win sympathy for you.'

'It's the grey in the beard,' we say.

But at length the great day comes; our stuff arrives by car.

Unpacking and reorganizing—driving picture-hooks into the plaster of our walls to put up photographs, discovering cutlery, tableware we'd packed away so many months ago and which all seem to belong to another world—takes two more days. But we begin to feel we've arrived.

There's a new problem now, though. Our radiators are still cold and, as the snow drifts down outside the windows, the lack of heating is beginning to feel a bit alarming. Maybe there won't be any all winter? It isn't only in our house. Whole regions of the city are without heat and many families, including Olga's, have no hot water. I worry about Vanya with his bad attacks of asthma.

One of the men who does repair work in this building goes off and buys us a small fan heater. He's immensely proud of his succesful expedition, but sadly the heater makes a lot of noise but produces little heat. And if we have any other electrical appliance on when we use it, we are liable to be plunged into darkness. The electrical system in the building doesn't like being overloaded. The electric kettle is a particular source of trouble. More than once, all power fades as the kettle boils, and we eat a half-warmed up supper by candlelight.

Things cheer up when a radiator comes on in our living-room. Nothing in the bedroom, which is also my study, but we assure our disbelieving friends we're used to unheated bedrooms. The heating comes on in the school. Once again I learn how life here simply consists of doing without.

We also learn how Russians seal windows. Long strips of old sheets are stuck in place by a paste made of flour and water. The outside panes are done first, then the gap between the double panes of the windows. The double doors which lead on to our lopsided balcony are filled up with sawdust. Hamsters would have a good time here, Stuart says!

Then the inner frames are sealed. Only the *fortochka* is left unsealed. This is a little hinged window at the top of every casement of every home.

There are break-ins along our corridor, but no one gets into our room. We have a very secure lock, but the doors are so flimsy a single blow from an axe would break them in. However, we try not to think about that.

After the stress of the week at the port, Stuart gets an attack of flu. Hearing this, a friend comes with a jar of raspberry jam, honey, aspirins, potatoes and a jar of home-made pickled cabbage salad. We learn that raspberry jam in hot water is the Russian secret for bringing down a temperature. It works, too!

I'm busy with the children. Sonia wants to hold a poetry evening. The sixth class—the eleven-year-olds—will recite the poems of the favourite Russian poet, Alexander Pushkin. Pushkin is for Russia what Burns is for Scotland, and more—not just a poet, but a national myth.

The eighth class are going to major on the work of Aleksei Tolstoy, and the tenth class, which includes me since I join them for their literature lessons, will focus on Marina Tsvetaeva, a poet forbidden until recently in the USSR and certainly never studied in Soviet schools.

In each case the children will not only recite poems, but trace the development of the poet's life and work and sing poems set to music. One of the teachers will sing a poem about Pushkin written by a child in the sixth class which he himself has set to music and accompanies on the guitar.

It sounds a nice programme. Everyone works hard, including me, learning my poem off by heart, which is something I could never do in English. Russian poetry is more rhythmic than English and perhaps this helps. As I go up and down slow-moving escalators, squash into overcrowded public transport, carry bags of bread and cabbage and whatever vegetables I'm able to find being sold on the streets, I recite to myself Tsvetaeva's words about her poems being like vintage wines which will come into their own one day.

The evening seems to be a great success. Everyone performs well, parents attend. There's a good atmosphere.

So why do three men, all members of the Society, get up in the middle and walk out?

Why does the deputy headmaster of the school tell Sonia the younger children can't possibly have a free period next morning and then, when it's all over and they've all gone home, turn to her and say that they can?

Why is it left to Stuart to thank Sonia and the children for their hard work?

We sense bad feelings among the leadership this evening. A hint of chill... We do not know it, but worse is to come.

The next day we need cheese so I head out for the shops, armed with the essential polythene bag, but forgetting the jam jar I will need if I see some sour cream.

The workman who bought us the fan heater meets me on my way downstairs and says, 'I congratulate you on the end of the world!' A group of people have apparently been handing out lurid leaflets predicting the end of the world on 28 October. There's a story that one poster read: The end of the world is the 28th—we'll meet on the 29th at our usual address.

I go out into the muddy street. Snow falls and melts, leaving puddles everywhere. I walk along Old Nevsky Prospekt. Queues are forming outside shut shops. Is it lunch-time or not? Some shops shut from 1–2, others from 2–3 — and others again from 3–4.

I'm not left long to wonder. Almost as soon as I'm inside the food shop, wondering which counter to choose for cheese (or should I go to the till first and save an extra wait in a queue?) a young thug puts his arms forcibly around me and ejects me.

'Dinner time!' he says, by way of explanation.

I'm very shaken; angry too; but turn away and go to the Finnish shop, an overcrowded supermarket where at least there are things to buy—in currency. There's a big bully-boy standing by the door here too—to guard the precious currency products. I spend 65 Finn marks—and give £10. You have to be an economist here to work out all the rates of exchange.

I don't buy cheese in the Finnish shop, hoping to get some for roubles. I cross the road, and from a stall buy a carton of milk (hoping it won't go sour), sour cream in a soft polythene bag, good tomatoes, a bottle of fizzy orange (Austrian). I cross back, and see a thermos! Sonia has broken hers. It's absolutely essential for life here and there don't seem to be any for sale anywhere. This one costs 350 roubles. I haven't enough. I try to work out exchange rates and offer the woman a dollar, which she has no trouble accepting. She tells me the thermos comes from the Baltic republics. It's the last one and she's selling it cheaper because there's a mark on the side.

I head home, but see mayonnaise in a booth on the way and spend my last fifty roubles on it. The man putting a bell on our door carries my bags upstairs for me—this is the nicer side to Russian life.

I find visitors with Stuart. We don't have to move far ourselves—the whole world comes to our room.

But I have to go to the Institute where we teach evening courses in English. We talk about festivals. I play carols from King's College Chapel, talk about Christmas, write poems on the rough blackboard, using the faint crumbly chalk. The girls who attend the class say they love hearing poetry—they've only ever read English poetry in Russian. We talk about Hallowe'en. I feel sad at being so far away from home, especially when a girl talks about Christmas being a special time for the family.

I travel back by metro, cross the dimly-lit road and to my apprehension find a dark figure sitting on the landing of the unlit stairs. He's an old man, obviously a bit simple; one of the city's homeless. He tells me he's just resting here. I send Stuart down with bread and meat from a tin we'd opened. He tries to get the old man to leave, but in vain. After all, if your home is the street, a landing on the stairs is to be preferred. I warn Stuart there'll be puddles on the floor. Next morning there are—and worse... It's a good thing Stuart put a spade in our luggage!

15

South to the Caucasus: Kislovodsk

The snow had been whirling in blizzards since mid-October. But, like the swallows, Sonia, Vladik, her ten-year-old son (my godson) and I went south. Yes, the holiday we planned as we went out of town to visit Mitya in his army camp had come true. It was the school half-term and we were getting away from it all. Away from the tensions in the Society, away from the snow in St Petersburg, away from our menfolk too, who came to the station to see us off.

We travelled in a very cold carriage which warmed up as the train trundled south at a pace so sedate you could count the tree-tops. Stuart looked at me with such pity as he kissed me goodbye. 'I feel so sorry for you, going off for two whole days in the train,' he murmured, with real sadness in his eyes.

I could hardly believe my ears. 'But I love train journeys! I'm really looking forward to it.'

It was 6p.m. on a snowy dark Friday—31 October. Hallowe'en. We wouldn't arrive in Kislovodsk, in the north Caucasus, until 2.30 on Sunday, travelling from the same latitude as southern Shetland to a latitude, Stuart tells me, about the same as the middle of Italy.

And I knew I would love every minute. A good long train journey prepares you for the arrival. And Russian trains have class. Of a sort.

I remembered student days travelling to Poland, how I'd walk along the corridor to Russian carriages with a samovar arrangement at the end of each wagon, and a formidable looking lady in charge.

It was my dream, even then, to travel on a long-distance Russian train. I'd love to go on the Trans-Siberian railway. Sonia tells me one day I must go with her to Sasha's home town of Vladivostok, a week's journey by train right across Russia, and I assure her I'd like nothing better.

But I'd hope for a nicer lady in charge. The one on this journey was unpleasant. She seemed to enjoy getting into fights with everyone! Sonia and I shut the compartment door and kept mousey quiet. We were in our own compartment with four bunks—you lift the bottom ones to stow away your bags.

We wondered who our extra person would be, but he was a young student with pals down the corridor and he came in only to stretch out on the top bunk and sleep, refusing tea and coffee even though we offered it.

There was a restaurant car, but the prices were too dear. Sonia had cooked a chicken and hard-boiled eggs. I added apples and sausage and—real luxury—half an Orkney cheese, which had travelled with our luggage and was none the worse for being three months or so at sea.

We had bread with us, but were able to top up our supplies whenever we needed, because when the train pulled in at a station for any length of time (it could be anything from ten minutes to half an hour), peasant women and men would come swarming round the train with fresh warm buns, buckets of apples and tubs of cream. There was hot drinking water on tap for most of the journey. Russians would bring a small teapot, brew up strong tea and keep topping that up for the journey. Sonia and I had tea and coffee in bags—not my favourite way of brewing either beverage, but useful for the journey.

To Vladik's delight, there were also sellers of ice-cream and we bought some twice.

We woke up next morning to find we were trundling through Ukraine at a pace so slow you could count the birch trees. The temperature rose. If the train stopped for half an hour, we'd take it in turns to walk up the platform, one of us always left in charge of our things. We were in the last coach of eighteen which was bad for buying things because the peasants with their buckets of apples and tubs of cream had sold out by the time we arrived mid-platform.

The countryside was flat, miles of forests, fields largely under water, glimpses of small towns and villages with wooden houses, no paved roads, few wheeled vehicles of any kind, apart from occasional bicycles. Our huge train would pull up at small out-of-the-way places, and people with bundles on their backs would pick their way across the railway tracks and disappear into the vastness of the countryside, heading for home.

The next morning again we awoke to rolling countryside, a feel of the south, black-hatted shepherds on horseback, and heat.

We stopped at one place. A thermometer read an incredible thirty-one degrees. We stripped off all we could. I had to borrow a short-sleeved blouse from Sonia. I stepped out onto the platform, shaking slightly from the motion of the train but feeling very summery, very away from it all.

People now began to look very southern, Spanish, gypsy-like too. I walked past groups of women and girls with thick, black hair tumbling over their shoulders, bright clothes. I watched people in their houses, a woman brushing her front doorstep. It was fairly run down, but so bright and sunny.

This truly was another world!

An absolutely filthy train with broken windows drew alongside ours, going from Baku, former Soviet Asia, to Moscow. Sonia said disapprovingly, 'They let it get into a mess and blame us Russians for the state of things.' Our own coach became a little less convenient as the tyrant tea lady locked one of the two toilets, and the remaining one became slightly less than savoury.

The landscape changed. There were bright flowers round the little wooden houses we passed, trees in leaf along the dusty roads. Mountains rose dramatically out of flat countryside, one of them amazingly like Arthur's Seat in Edinburgh but without the Pentland Hills.

We felt hotter than ever as we started to bundle our things together. We were at our destination, Kislovodsk.

We pulled in at a clean, neat station. Carrying our bags the length of the platform gave us a chance to survey the train which had brought us so far. We came out into the town square, crossed the road and took the bus a couple of stops to the hotel where Sonia and Vladik stayed when they first came here, when Vladik was four and was recovering from a winter of asthma. To restore him to health Sonia taught evening courses so that she could stay at home with Vladik during the day, taking him out for a daily walk, massaging him and cupping him (putting heated glasses on his back to break up the phlegm in his lungs). Then she brought him on a visit here to take the waters.

This time we weren't staying in a hotel—costs were too high. Friends had booked us in with a landlady. Our room was on the top (fifth) floor of a block of flats tucked in among trees with a view front and back of rolling hills. Everything was clean and neat—and small. I kept wondering whether this really could be Russia! I liked the place enormously. The air is the purest in the former Soviet Union. Breathing felt like drinking fresh water. The place was a fashionable nineteenth-century resort where Russians 'took the waters'. It was immortalized by Mikhail Lermontov in the novel Sonia had brought with her for us to read on the train: *Hero of Our Time.*

We went out to experience the local mineral water, which is called *narzan*. We went downhill along an avenue lined with evergreens to a hexagonal building with a fountain which had a series of taps in the middle.

And there everyone was, all the local people, filling their jugs and bottles and drinking the water. It had a taste vaguely like bad eggs, but it was cold and fizzy. Kislovodsk is now the last spa in Russia, and even here tourism is dying, so local young people can no longer hope for hotel work. People are afraid to come here now because of the unrest on all the borders. Sonia noticed a heavy police presence. And during our stay there was a murder, with a whole family wiped out, much talked about in this small town. It was a mafia job; the man had traded on the local market for years. But we didn't see any sign of any trouble.

We phoned Sasha with the news of our safe arrival and left Vladik to watch television with the landlady, a childish soul who liked the same cartoons as him. And Sonia and I went to the baths, the *banya*, to relax after our train journey, and to get ready to take the waters. In fact, I've never had so many baths in my life! Sanatoria have sprung up everywhere in the town. Each place of work runs one. So there's the factory workers' sanatorium, the teachers' sanatorium, firemen's... and so on. People used to be given paid leave to come here and 'rest', as the Russians call having a holiday. Or you could go as members of a family. So, because Sasha is in the Army, we all set off to the sanatorium run by the Red Army for its soldiers and their families.

'You're my godmother,' said Vladik, 'that's the same as family.'

Sonia and I weren't so sure that particular kinship tie was one which would be acknowledged by the Red Army.

'We'll book you in as Yevgenia,' said Sonia. 'But what shall we use for a patronymic. What was your father's name?'

'William...'

But we agreed that wouldn't do. 'My grandfather was Peter,' I volunteered.

So I was Yevgenia Petrovna who had lived a long time in Poland! Luckily, apart from a chatty cloakroom lady, no one asked questions.

The whole place was spick and span, cleaner than anything I'd seen in St Petersburg. But then, I had not moved in the exalted circles of the Red Army, hadn't seen how the other half live...

The cleanliness was maintained by women with besom brooms.

We waited outside a room with baths in curtained-off cubicles. A nurse with a white coat, red hair and long earrings dangling beneath the tall chef's hat which is the uniform of medical workers in Russia ran a bath for me and I lay and soaked in the mineral water, silky and soft, with little bubbles of *narzan* welling up around me. An egg-timer told me when my ten minutes were up.

All the top brass of the Red Army—even Yeltsin—come here to get their backs rubbed, and clear their smoke-filled lungs with various inhalers. But because it was off-season, we got everything laid on for us: the daily bath in *narzan*, a massage of the spine and an underwater massage.

So, having pulled on my clothes after the first soak, I went upstairs and took almost all of them off again, in order to lie on a couch for a massage of the spine, given by a partially sighted lady. It was a marvellous sensation to give myself totally into a healer's hands. Vladik got a *narzan* bath and hung around, a bit bored, while Sonia and I had our massage and sat quietly for a few minutes afterwards, sipping the *narzan* we brought in a bottle with us each day.

Then we walked in the park—hilly, and vast. It reminded me so much of Scotland, with dark pine trees stretching around the shoulders of rolling hills. Red squirrels fed from Vladik's hand, to his indescribable joy; blue tits too.

Other days we'd go into the pleasant little town—it's all downhill—strolling past small shops, gypsy street sellers. None of the awful misery and despair of St Petersburg. I was repeatedly reminded of Portugal. There were even small cafés, and we'd sit with a cup of coffee and ice cream; or we'd buy bread, gorgeous buns. So we didn't lose any weight in spite of the underwater massage, which happened every day at 12.30. That was something! You lie in a small pool, holding the side, and the nurse turns on a hosepipe. She works her way up from toes to ankles, calves, knees, across your stomach, then you turn over and she hoses the small of your back. Sonia said it's to break up kidney stones, and I can well believe it might.

The nurse asked me to sit up, and turned the hosepipe on my arms and shoulders. Since I'm a bit puny in comparison with most Russian women I had to ask her to reduce the flow! I emerged from the massage red all over and feeling totally relaxed, but quite tired too. I wished Stuart could have been there to experience the therapy.

But his not being there meant I spoke only Russian. And that gave my language an enormous boost. Sonia was punctillious about keeping language lessons going. I carried a notebook everywhere and as we walked through the park or the town I took care to note down phrases and vocabulary. It made a pleasant souvenir of our time in Kislovodsk when I came to revise the work later.

I worked on the language, too, reading the New Testament in Russian, stretched out on the bed. In the evenings, Sonia either worked with me or chatted up the landlady, a lonely soul in her mid-fifties, who was always in bed by 9p.m., and left before 7a.m. to work as a cleaner in the sanatorium. That was until the weekend of the Great October Revolution (7 November, still being celebrated as a holiday here, though it goes almost unnoticed now in St Petersburg). Our landlady didn't come home then for two nights!

Sonia was almost out of her mind. I felt decidedly uneasy too. Suppose she had been murdered and we had to call the police? Here was I, paying in roubles instead of staying in a hotel paying fifty dollars a night, as foreigners should. We couldn't think what to do. The lady had told us she was a widow, with two grown-up children, one in the Urals, the other in Murmansk. Eventually, feeling very nosey and unhappy about doing so, we discovered and opened her address book—and found her certificate of divorce. So the bit about being a widow wasn't quite true.

We tried the first number and were in luck. It was someone who'd worked in the same sanatorium as our landlady for thirty-six years. 'Don't worry,' she said, 'she'll come back from her lady friend!'

We deduced she'd been out drinking. Yet nothing in her lifestyle made this seem likely, and when she finally turned up on the very morning of our departure she was as fresh and rosy as if nothing had happened.

That was the only worry in a relaxing holiday.

There were marked paths through the park. We took different routes each day. Once we went up in a cable-car. That was fantastic! We swung out over pine trees, with views down to the town beneath us, where the street lights had just come on, and to the snow-capped mountains away in Southern Caucasus. The peak of the highest and most beautiful of all, Mount Elbruz (where some British climbers almost came to grief the following April) rose breathtakingly into the sunset sky.

We came back to earth with reluctance, to the appetising smell of *shashliks*. People were eating out of doors in the almost intoxicatingly heady air, and drinking red wine.

We wished we could join them, but I'd let Stuart talk me into going off with only 6,000 roubles (then £6), half of which went on our ten days' lodging. We tried to change Western money, but few foreign visitors come to Kislovodsk and the exchange place in the hotel had closed at the end of the summer.

So we were short of cash. It did me good to be like all my Russian friends: to look at cartons of juice, jars of chocolate spread I longed to buy for Vladik—and have no means of purchasing such goodies. But I was sorry, because a very little hard currency would have gone a long way and I wanted to give Sonia a holiday and take us all out for meals and other treats. Instead she husbanded our resources very carefully and the only meals out we allowed ourselves were dumplings in a little local restaurant.

But I managed to change my only Western money, ten dollars, at a stall in the market which bore a card saying: 'I buy dollars.' Luckily for us, a gentle Eastern lady was in charge—not any of the wide boys who could easily have made off with my dollars, giving nothing in return. So, armed with bundles of grubby notes, we sallied forth to purchase woollen goods. It was snowing that day and countrywomen anxious to get home reduced their prices. They were selling mohair sweaters for £1.50! How I wished I had more money! I was in sore need of boots, and this was certainly the place to buy them. But I bought a big jar of honey instead.

The snow didn't last. The weather turned balmy again. Next time we went to the market it was to stock up for the winter. Sonia bought 10 kilos of onions, 6 kilos of garlic, 1 kilo of walnuts. I bought walnuts too, and hazelnuts, although we don't have nutcrackers. Then I sat and looked at life while Sonia went off to a covered market for meat. Non-Russian languages were being spoken around me—Uzbek, perhaps, or Georgian. But most people were local peasants selling the produce they'd grown themselves, or hazelnuts they'd gathered from trees in the hills round about. Sonia bought the fat side of pig (no meat) which she and Vladik salted that evening, laying garlic between the layers. All this of course had to be carried back to St Petersburg, together with apples and pears which the family hadn't tasted for years.

Kislovodsk would certainly be on my travel itinerary in future, and I'd urge any of my friends who came to Russia to try to get south to the Caucasus and take the waters in the beautiful new hotel which was opening up close to our lodgings.

I kept thinking: why don't we do Bible teaching here? There's one Orthodox church for the whole town. I twice saw white-robed missionaries with cloths round their heads, like shepherds in a Nativity play, but in all that vast countryside we trundled home across I saw churches in only one Ukrainian city.

16

Plastering Over the Cracks

Last night, as he was getting into bed, Stuart said, 'That's plaster falling.'

I reassured him. 'No, it's that packet of felt-tip pens at the end of the bed. You must have kicked them off.'

But it wasn't. It was plaster. Another dollop fell later, waking me up—and I lay there until 4a.m. listening to our ceiling falling down. In the end I woke Stuart up.

'You were right about the plaster, Stuart. The ceiling's falling down.'

'I'm asleep,' he said helpfully.

But I was wide awake—mind racing. What should we do? Was the ceiling coming down, or was it just the plaster which had been put over the enormous crack down the middle drying out? Was there any point putting more plaster on? Suddenly the phrase 'plastering over the cracks' had a new and terrible meaning.

That's just what's happening here. People plaster over cracks all the time. The whole infrastructure's been ruined. Nature is one swamp of pollution. The economy's in ruins, in spite of the gloss put on to try to attract Big Business. The social structure's in ruins. And our house is falling down.

Like Henny Penny, Ducky Lucky—the ridiculous names ran in my mind along with a vivid memory of that painting in the Russian museum, *The Last Days of Pompeii*, in which everyone is sheltering everyone else as their city collapses around them.

No one was sheltering me.

I tried again. 'Stuart...'

Growl...

'Stuart, you must get up, please, Stuart and look at the crack.'

'What good will that do?' he demanded. But he got up, trekked through to the other room and came back with a broom. He gave the plaster a poke and got back into bed.

'We're still here,' he said next morning when we both woke up.

Yes, but only just. For in our Society everyone is falling out with everyone else, dismissing people from teaching, handing jobs over with no warning to other people. Tears flow, doors slam. People who have been friends for twenty years hurl insults at each other. One man even threatens to punch another up and has to be physically held back.

People feel Boris has become a new Tsar. 'We were all in this together,' they say. 'Now you're trying to run it for yourself.'

Boris comes to offload his view on Stuart. 'We've got this building; we've got to organize, manage it, work, work, work. They don't know how hard we have to work.'

And he's right, of course. He's been abroad, he's seen wider horizons, and he and Lena are the ones who fight and hassle in the town councils to keep hold of the building, and have to pay the workers who vainly try to keep it from falling down.

'I'm going to have to take a firm hand,' he concludes, his face set. 'They'll have to do what I say whether they agree or not.'

Who are 'they'? It becomes too obvious. The three men who walked out of the poetry evening.

'The school isn't stretching the children enough,' they say. 'The teachers aren't up to the mark.'

'Sonia is,' I protest.

'But that evening of poetry of hers. It was too Soviet. She put those children on show as though they were all Young Pioneers.'

So that's why they had walked out... and then gone on to organize their own literary evening. Three men and one woman whose grandchildren are both in the school had organized a series of Russian literature lectures, without consulting Sonia, who accepted it all very meekly. I'd dutifully gone to one of the lectures but I hadn't been able to understand the usual quick, muttered Russian. Nor had I liked to see the young people in the tenth class, who were being targeted for this special approach, being used as pawns in the quarrels of adults.

'We like the new seminars,' they said, but I think they simply felt flattered.

They became very dismissive of Sonia and cool with me, very aware of their position as the new intellectual élite.

Perhaps it's all growing pains. It's hard for us, in the middle. And it's very hard for everyone involved to see a good thing torn apart from within.

In the middle of all this, Stuart has a three-day deacons' course to prepare for and teach. It's held out of town in the newly-built Lutheran church he went to last September. All pine and glass, clean: even the water's clean. Our water here is like the goldfish bowl when it's time to empty it. We boil water to drink, but even so a scum forms on the bottom of the jars we fill every day, there being no taps in our room.

Vladimir, a pastor in the Finnish Lutheran Church, has set up these courses. He's suffered for his faith, getting chucked out of the college because he was a believer, and being forced to serve in very harsh conditions in the Army—so harsh that a stammer he'd been cured of through prayer returned; a severe handicap. He's a good teacher and preacher. I never fail to benefit from his studies and sermons. People come from far and wide to attend the courses, some getting up before 5a.m. each day to travel into town, arriving back late at night.

'It makes a nice change from all the quarrels here,' I tell Stuart.

Quarrels—yes, they are still going on. For ten days now people have been firing one another, calling endless meetings, walking out in anger. Peace talks are being organized—Stuart has been given the unenviable position of official mediator. The trouble is that everyone comes from a background of dissent, without any experience at working normally. No one has been able to have an unprejudiced view of life, and now they've started too much too soon.

Sonia laments—to begin a good thing and tear it apart with their own hands!

Money, it may be, and power even more, has had a corrupting influence. There are accusations of mismanagement of finances. To make matters worse, pupils and teachers are related, so people are forming camps—and, besides, they're Russians! That sounds racist, but they say it themselves, bitterly.

'It's the Russian character,' Anastasia, who teaches English, explains. 'We love tragedy. We don't know the centre path, the golden mean.' Anastasia's English is impeccable. She comes to us in tears, heartbroken at the rift she sees.

'I thought Boris was someone I could utterly trust, but not now. I don't know what to do, I don't know which side to choose,' she sobs.

Meantime Sonia and I are rehearsing the Russian Nativity play we've been asked by Lena and the other teachers to put on at the end of term with the children. I particularly want to do it because the last day of term is 25 December, so the play will have special meaning for me.

It's the first ever Russian Nativity play. The big Orthodox festival is Easter. Even pre-Revolution, the type of theatre which was performed at Christmas had more in common with mummers and slapstick than with religion. Or so people tell me. Everyone seems suddenly very knowledgeable about old traditions which have been neglected for three generations. There seem to be very few, if any, traditional Russian Christmas carols. Aida lends us a Baptist hymn-book in which the carols have all been translated from German or even English. Stuart and I have fun going over some old favourites, such as the Russian version of 'Hark the herald angels sing'.

Nastya in the eighth class, who sings in a church choir, comes up with one or two Russian carols and rehearses some of the girls herself after school. All the teachers of the younger classes who have nothing to do with the quarrels in the Society are very interested and slightly incredulous about this play.

And while his uncle, the deputy director, creates havoc among the staff, the nephew, a pupil in the eighth class, is breaking hearts and producing tears and poetry among the girls. Life, as Stuart says, is never dull.

Our nights aren't dull either. If it isn't the sound of plaster falling, it's the rustle and scraping of mice. We brought a cat to the room. I made up some powdered milk. Russian cats have forgotten what fish and real milk taste like. It lapped up the milk, curled up and slept, but got out when the door was open and it has never come back. The mice are running along the top of the wood panelling. Action is needed. Another cat.

Then comes a Society meeting in which forty-five members walk out. This is followed by a teachers' meeting at which there is so much plain animosity that I shrivel up inside. (It reminded me of the time when I was visiting a family in one of our parishes, and the wife threw a butcher's cleaver at her husband.)

In the midst of all this two angelic-looking brothers from Taizé visit, highlighting the tragedy of what we're living through. Stuart has had hours of peacekeeping talk, day and night. The kids in the tenth class gleefully join the fight and stage a strike. Who knows how it will end? Parents have joined the battle too, but Sonia and I have decided we're going to ignore it all and get on with the Nativity Play.

We use Old Testament texts and the Luke and Matthew tellings of the Nativity and intersperse this with a poem by Pasternak and some free narrative, like the innkeeper saying, 'There's no room. Go away.' The kids in the sixth and eighth class who will do this play like this bit and say it with gusto.

But now we stumble on a big problem. Nastya, our singer, who has been elevated to a very important role as musical expert and religious adviser, tells us that she's feeling worried about the play.

'No one is worthy to play the Mother of God,' she declares. Even worse, she's sure Orthodox tradition is against any portrayal of the Virgin or of Christ on stage.

Sonia, as ever, finds a way out. The children who play Mary and Joseph won't have speaking parts. They'll form a tableau. The other children will be narrators, a kind of chorus. And Mary's sayings, which have been lifted straight from the Bible, will be taken by different girls so that no one person can be said to be playing the part. Nastya herself, with her lovely, mature singing voice, will sing the Magnificat in Slavonic.

So rehearsals continue, and Sonia puts hours of her own time into this play, almost as if she feels it's a way of saving the Society.

But the rift only deepens. Stuart is still the official mediator—and it's not at all easy to be in the middle in a situation where, as in the old days, 'if you're not for us, you're against us'; and everyone swears the other is wrong, sick, is a liar. How will it all end?

Similar struggles are going on in the government.

'Never mind,' the head of the college which meets along our corridor says to Stuart, darkly. 'We'll soon be out of here.'

So they're planning to take all the students off to another building. Why set up peace talks, when all too clearly, there's no will? On either side? Never mind! That's the key to survival. Things fall apart; but, never mind.

So—never mind—I'm making a Christmas cake. Dough mingles with Stuart's Greek dictionaries on our only table (but never mind) and I wrap the cake tin in brown paper, put trays of water under it and watch our temperamental cooker carefully so that it doesn't burn the outside and undercook the middle.

We're still being attacked by mosquitoes. They seem to live in all the nooks and crannies, not least, perhaps, in the bathroom where the steam must help them thrive. When I occasionally faint-heartedly tackle long undisturbed dirt, mosquitoes fly out—but never mind!

17

The Wall of Hatred

It's a week before Christmas. At nine o'clock this morning we watched the first light of day streak the sky behind our window. Light spread, reddened. There would be some sun today, though there was a sharp frost. I went out to the Lavra Church to buy Christmas cards.

As usual I forget that there will be a line of beggars. I see a young man with cerebral palsy who often sits there in his wheelchair. I give him money, but I say, *Zdrastvuyte*—and our eyes meet. I'm ashamed, and on the way back I stop to talk to him. He jumps, startled, then his face lights up. It's cold, and he's in thin jeans. I say, 'It's cold for you, sitting here.' 'I have to,' he says. I ask him if he lives alone. He says, 'No, in a house.' I dread to think what kind of house it is that drives him out into the frost to beg. I say, 'May God keep you,' and he puts the whole of his strength into an attempt at a wave as I walk away. I've given him one rouble—but spend 1,000 roubles on stamps for our overseas Christmas cards.

The usual unsavoury crowd of wide boys hangs about the hotel. I think of the misery of the beggars, the little old ladies who plead, 'Give a babushka some mercy!' A child goes running with kopecks to each one, receiving a smile, a word of thanks, a blessing.

There's a meeting to discuss the Nativity play, the tea which will follow, the concert, costumes and dances, all on 25 December.

My head feels as though it's been machine-gunned with a torrent of words.

Some little girls want to give us a kitten, but Stuart says a firm no. He caught a mouse—a young one—in the trap this morning. Perhaps because I'm reading *Crime and Punishment*, it seems preferable to have a cat to keep the mice at bay, rather than commit murder...

Murder of a different sort is being committed here—and who'd be a peacekeeper? Lena, the target of everyone's criticism, came to us asking Stuart to respond to a letter from abroad. The person who handles foreign correspondence has locked all documents away and is refusing to let Boris and Lena get their hands on any. So when it became known that Stuart had helped Lena he got called a traitor by the opposing side.

In this spirit of peace and goodwill to all we get on with our lives! Sonia gave the children an essay—a quotation apparently found in a church in France—'Does the wall of hatred reach to heaven?' Twelve-year-old Asya wrote, 'Jesus said, "Treat others as you would like them to treat you." If people don't love each other, but hate one another they cannot know God or be with him and therefore for them the wall of hatred does reach to heaven.' Sonia showed this piece to Lena at the teacher's meeting. She made no comment. By now it's 10p.m.—I'm still reading *Crime and Punishment*. The murderer and the prostitute read the Raising of Lazarus—and she says, 'Go to the crossroads and bow down three times and kiss the earth which you have violated, and confess your crime.'

In class we wonder whether any other nineteenth-century book can be compared with this, and Sonia and I decide that much major twentieth-century literature reflects Raskolnikov: the anti-hero.

The Saturday before Christmas, I go shopping. I want to buy candlesticks for our Christmas table—but what craziness to choose a Saturday afternoon! The shopping arcade, Gostiny Dvor, is jam-packed—like Princes Street the Saturday before Christmas, only there's no tinsel. No one is laden down with things, people look, but don't buy. There's no hint that Christmas is near—except outside the foreign currency shop, always ready to lure tourists, where miserable little stickers say 'Merry Christmas' in English and 'With the Birth of Christ' in Russian.

I struggle through the crowds, often brought to a standstill, always jostled on all sides. There are far more Western than Soviet goods on sale in this shopping arcade which was once a showcase for the good life under socialism. Some counters offer goods for currency—a display of consumerism at which most Russians can only look with amazement, and envy. Others offer imported goods for roubles and I, ever at a loss with rows of noughts, buy tea for currency, and six crystal glasses—at about £18 for the set. I go home to find that the shortbread I'd left in the oven under Stuart's care has burnt at the bottom.

He said, 'It started to burn, but you told me it had to stay in till four o'clock, so I left it.'

One day, I guess we'll learn how to regulate this oven!

On the Fourth Sunday in Advent (Western Calendar), I coax the twin-tub into action, trying not to let it get to me too much. Soviet industry could send men—and a woman—into space, but can't provide washing-machines to make life easier for millions of families.

We go off to church and then out to Olga's.

On the way to the metro, Stuart and I pause to look at books on one of the stands on Nevsky Prospekt. This is a mistake. As we move away from the stall we're immediately hassled by four or five teenagers who waggle T-shirts in front of us. 'Five dollars, five dollars,' they chant, derisively. They try to separate us from one another, to snatch my bag from my shoulder, and twice manage to unfasten its strap. It's beginning to get very unpleasant. And in all this crowd no one wants to know. But then, what would we do if we saw two people being mobbed? Luckily the metro is close by and we finally shake them off—but feel very upset.

We stand the whole way (nothing unusual) then catch a bus, in which, amazingly, there's a free seat. Stuart gallantly offers it to me and I'm glad to sink onto it. I watch the rows of lit windows of block after housing block and feel safer here than on the main Nevsky Prospekt.

Olga is baking when we arrive. Vanya is brandishing a small hammer for cracking nuts. 'I would hit them with my hammer,' he declares, hearing about our misfortune. But Olga is in tears. A friend of hers, a singer, Konstantin Ivanov, was mugged and had his throat cut yesterday in his own home in front of his wife and five children.

Talk constantly comes back to this tragedy—but soon centres around the troubles in the Society and I find myself in tears, too. But everyone, even warm-hearted Olga, just says, 'It's our life, you have to accept our life.' We feel a solution is further away than ever.

'What will happen to us if the whole thing breaks up?' I ask Olga.

'You can come here. That bed-settee is waiting for you.' And we know she means it.

She talks about the times of danger and hardship in the past. 'But there was love,' she says, with her eyes full of tears.

I recall how she has endured house searchings, separation, loss, endless treks across Russia, to take things to the husband she was never allowed to see, her little daughters growing up, knowing their father only from rare letters, he knowing them only from their childish drawings, 'Dear daddy, we love you'... their photographs...

The wall of hatred, of separation, couldn't part this family, who became the focus of prayers in many countries, many languages, many different church denominations.

Next day a sickle moon cuts the dawn sky—the red sky glows above the golden dome. It's 9.15a.m. At lunch Lena tells me enthusiastically about the marvellous decorations the kids have done for the end of term. She sits with one of the teachers talking about invitation cards—as though there were no conflict, as though everything was happening normally.

In the evening two different sessions—attended by the two

rival groups—happen in the same building. Stuart and I are told about neither, and invited to neither. Perhaps it's just as well. Meantime Sonia and I have rehearsed our play with the kids yet again and I feel it's never going to be right. Half of them don't turn up; others have dropped out; our Virgin Mary has gone off sick. Christmas is four days away.

A phone call comes. Igor the captain whose boat has been stranded in the port of Leith, has been flown home with other members of the crew—but without his ship, which still has four boxes and two trunks of ours on board. Or rather, Igor assures us, safely locked away in the harbour. Will we ever get them? Igor is optimisitic.

He and his wife invite us round to their flat. He's full of his time in Scotland. A grim time it was too, stuck on a little tub way out in Leith Docks, but he said when they arrived in Moscow they all had the feeling: let's go back. Three of the younger crew members, from Ukraine and Riga, chose to stay. 'They got housed straight away,' says Igor. 'They were offered three-apartment flats and said, "This is too much, just give us one room." But they were told, "We only have three-apartment flats",' he ends with much laughter.

He talks about roads 'smooth as this table', praised the care that is taken of the elderly. 'Here,' he says, 'people in wheelchairs are left in their flats with nothing to do except stare out of the window.'

Other crew members are equally complimentary. A woman tells us how she and another crew member were out for a walk near the docks one evening when a young punk with a mohican and heavy chains rode along the pavement on his bike. 'I was quite scared. I stood back for him. And he said, "thank you". Imagine: thank you! I told my mother about it,' she went on. 'She has known only hardship all her life,' she adds, sorrowfully. 'She lived through the war, through starvation. She buried two of her children. And I said, "Just across the North Sea there's a country where people live differently." My mother couldn't believe me,' she concluded.

Another man said: 'We were taught: England is a capitalist country. They're all bad there. But no one says things like that now. Those old days have gone for ever.'

Yet still we're finding that people don't trust one another. In every group of people with which we are involved—the Society, this crew, and even the church—there are plots and machinations and insinuations. Plenty of walls between people still have to be broken down. But one thing everyone's agreed on. From the sailors to the lecturers in the college they quote a nineteenth-century poet, Tyutchev who says: 'You can't understand Russia with your intellect, only with your heart, only with your soul.'

MID·WINTER

18

◗◖◗◖◗◖◗◖◗◖◗◖

A Christmas No One Keeps

It's 24 December—Christmas Eve. I decide I must put up some decorations. We've received a few Christmas cards and this brings warmth to our hearts, colour to our room, and attracts great interest among the visitors, not least the schoolchildren who always pop in and out. Christmas cards are almost unheard of here, and the ones which are being sold, in church kiosks only, are rather sombre and with only a few designs.

So I go shopping for greenery. The problem is: where should I go? I choose a metro route, emerge and, lo and behold, in the crowd of passers-by I see a woman carrying branches of pine. People don't talk to one another in the streets, but I go up to her and ask her where she got them. 'From the market,' she says, 'beside Vladmirskaya Metro Station.' It's my favourite corner of this city, so close to Dostoyevsky's house, right opposite the Vladmirskaya Church whose domes the writer chose to live beside.

I like the market, too. The stallholders come from Central Asia, Georgia, Armenia, from all over Russia, to sell their produce. So off I go. I buy mandarin oranges—'from Sochi', the lady who is selling them tells me; a thin cos lettuce from Tadzhikistan—what a treat to see green things again, though the lettuce was enormously expensive! No wonder few people shop in the market. There are never any queues, and many stallholders simply stand behind the produce they've brought so far, hoping someone will come and buy.

I add a cucumber to my bag, tomatoes, honey from a man with a big fur hat who measures the sticky substance from an enamel washing-up bowl into a glass jar. He tells me he's come with it from the Voronezh region. I buy white cheese, thick sour cream, nicer than anything that's sold in the state shops (and three times the price!). So we'll have a treat tomorrow.

Outside in the street I buy pine branches, heavy with cones.

I carry this load into the Vladimirskaya Church. You go through two sets of heavy doors, up one flight of stairs, through more doors, all hard to negotiate with hands full of pine branches and a heavy bag (including eggs wrapped precariously in a paper poke)—not least because you should cross yourself three times and bow at every stage.

The smell of incense has lingered from morning prayer. The church is warm with folk about their business, setting candles before the icons, praying for their friends. I then lug my bag home, feeling a warm sense of achievement... to find that Bela, the lady in the canteen, has remembered that it's our Christmas and has kindly given us a present: wooden beakers and a painted wooden plate. And a card with good wishes.

In the evening Stuart goes to a Finnish service. He's been asked to preach in Russian, a concession, we suppose. I choose instead the new Russian Reformed Episcopal service, held in our friend Sergei's flat.

On the way home as I change trains a girl of no more than fourteen, too drunk to stand, is hustled onto the train by a youngish man. He dumps her on a seat and leaves the train. She's completely blotto, slumped—alone. How will she get home? Where is home?

Stuart and I wrap presents to give to friends we've invited to come and share Christmas tomorrow. We prepare food: he cracks walnuts and hazelnuts with a hammer. His service was miserable, he says, formal and cold. Neither of us is feeling very happy, far from our family.

Towards midnight we open presents we packed last summer and brought with us.

On Christmas Day we set our table. The yard below is still dark. Lights etch the shape of the branches of the trees. I light two candles. We celebrate Holy Communion at the table which serves as desk, work-top and eating-place.

Sonia and Mitya phone with good wishes for our festival. Russian Christmas is still twelve days away. Mitya has to go on duty, but Sonia will come with Sasha and Vladik to share our celebration. We've invited another family too.

It's the last day of term. The tiny tots and seven-year-olds put on their Christmas show. They are dressed up beautifully like little frost fairies and stars. They sing and dance, recite poems in Russian, English, French.

Then it's our turn to present the nativity play. Since this is such a new event at an end-of-term concert in Russia, Sonia has asked Stuart to introduce it.

It is very well received. All the parents and friends who have gathered to watch the concert follow with great interest. They love it when the tiny children come on dressed as shepherds. The little six-year-old girl who plays the Virgin moves solemnly across the stage: her eyes are full of wonder. The beautiful singing of the Magnificat in Slavonic gives the whole thing an almost mystical aura.

So after all it goes well—though not without one or two mistakes, and tears from those who forgot their words. People say how interesting, how good to keep Christmas. For our friends who gather in our room for salads, ham from a tin, sherry and Christmas cake, this is the first time they've celebrated this feast. It's the first time they've drunk sherry. We have to explain you don't knock it back like vodka. But it's hard to convince them: people believe you haven't drunk a toast properly if anything is left in the glass. And it's the first time they've sung carols. 'Silent Night' in Russian is definitely the favourite.

The day is punctuated by phone calls to and from our family at home.

On Boxing Day I have a big clean-up and so do the students along the corridor, who are getting ready for an end-of-term party.

We're invited, but I've already asked Nadezhda to come here with her three girls. We've invited her husband too, but he's just returned from one of his disappearing acts and is sleeping off the consequences.

Nadezhda's elder daughter, Zhenya sees a boy she knows at the students' party and goes along the corridor. I find a dress for her to wear. I've been keeping it for her anyway, a little black number which used to belong to my daughter. She's delighted with it, and with a bra I find for her. But she's sullen with her mother.

Stuart goes off to see how the party's going and Nadezhda and I sit and talk while the two younger girls enjoy making things with glitter and pieces of straw.

Nadezhda has received the offer of promotion—her senior is emigrating to Israel. Her workplace provides vouchers for Littlewoods, and a colour television—so Nadezhda can sell hers—but it will bring in money. 'If you only knew,' she says, 'how hard life is financially.'

But that single room...

She says, 'There are families who live worse than us.'

I find it hard to believe.

Then it's time for us to snatch a three-day break away from the stresses and trauma of this last month. Sonia has arranged an empty flat for us through friends of friends down the electric line in Kolpina, the port built by Peter the Great. It's warm in the flat. We sleep. I soak in a clean bath, try to read *The Brothers Karamazov* in Russian. Stuart works on material for his deacons' course next week.

We go for a walk, slithering over snowy pavements. We eat ice-creams in a place... you can't call it a café. As we leave, a child comes in, a thin-faced, unwashed little boy of about seven, already streetwise. He's wearing a fur hat, no gloves. The cuffs of his thin jersey are worn and dirty. He tries to drain the dregs of Stuart's milk shake, scrape up smears of ice cream from my empty dish.

Like the beggar boy Dostoyevsky once saw, neglected, plainly in the pay of some group who sent him in thin clothes out on the streets to touch the pity of passers-by, he's a sad little symbol of the Christmas no one keeps.

The child Dostoyevsky met inspired a sketch for a Christmas story—'A Boy at Christ's Christmas Party'—in which, without naming the town, the author gives an exact picture of the Petersburg of the 1870s:

'Lord, what a town! He had never seen anything like it in his life. Where he'd come from it was so dark at night: only one light for a whole street. But there it was so warm, at least, and they gave him something to eat. But what noise here, what thunder, what light and people, horses and carriages. Frost, frost, frost! And steam coming from the muzzles of over-driven horses. Their hooves rang on the cobbles through the fine snow, and everyone shoving and pushing and Lord, how much he wanted to eat, even one bite of something...'

The child in this Christmas story finds a shelter behind some logs in a yard and falls asleep. In his dream Christ appears to him and invites him to his own Christmas party...

19

Historic Russia:
Yaroslavl and Rostov

I head for 'historic Russia' on a school trip with some of the sixth
and eighth classes. The kids have begged me to join them on this
trip, to parts of Russia few if any of them have had the chance to
see. Monasteries and churches would not have been on the agenda
of trips from any of their previous schools. Of course, I'm only too
glad to have the chance to go with them, to see a Russia I have only
minimally read about and never seen.

It's seventeen degrees below freezing. I'm swaddled in three
pairs of trousers, an underlining, a coat, scarf and gloves, so that,
like Russian toddlers swathed similarly in layers of clothing, I can
hardly move. 'Sweat breaks no bones,' as the Russians say.
Overheating and overeating are the thing. Or used to be. In these
days of power cuts, high prices, few people can afford even basic
foodstuffs.

We meet at Moscow Station, under Lenin's statue, which is
the meeting point for everyone who comes to this station. 'Meet
you at Lenin,' people say.

Our party numbers eighteen, with five adults: Alexei (the
class teacher), his wife Nadia (a musicologist), two mothers and
me. Our train is called the Volzhanka, meaning 'a female from the
River Volga region'. Our destination is the town of Yaroslavl,
where we'll sleep and eat in the Karl Marx school.

We have basic *platzkartni* tickets, which means an open coach
divided into sections of four seats together, two above two, and

145

across a narrow corridor a similar arrangement with single seats which make into a bed lengthwise. It's too bad if you have drunk or noisy neighbours.

Across the corridor sits a young woman who asks me what my native language is. She's hoping I'm French—a language she knows well. She's a student, married with a little girl, and she's going home to Yaroslavl for the New Year holidays. She tells me the history of the town.

Peopled by Finno-Ugrian tribes, it became Slavonic in the first years of the eleventh century. Prince Yaroslavl the Wise of Rostov (another historic town close by, which we would also visit) founded the town he honoured with his own name—and so gained control of the waterways of Central Russia, including the mighty Volga.

Yaroslavl was burnt by the Poles in the 'Troubled Times' at the beginning of the seventeenth century, when Polish invaders actually occupied Moscow. The buildings were all of wood and the town was razed to the ground, but the monastery and its walls were built of stone and remain to this day. The town's symbol is a golden bear with a sickle. I think, if I understood the story correctly, this is because in a skirmish with the local Finns a bear came to the rescue of the Slavs.

She doesn't mention—and I only learn later—that the first woman cosmonaut, Valentina Tereshkova, worked in a car factory in Yaroslavl. Not long ago, this would have been the main reason for visiting the town.

The beds on the train are hard, but we've slept—or most of us have. Another Valentina with her daughter Zhenya were in a section with noisy neighbours and Valentina didn't sleep at all. It's a sign of the times that there's no tea for sale. But there is hot water, and I have tea bags. We eat some biscuits and feel very glad of having a lining inside us on arrival as we hump our luggage through deep snow.

I seem to have far more luggage than anyone else—and my rucksack with handles and straps and clasps stands out among the khaki boy-scout variety on everyone else's backs. We go to the trolleybus stop outside the station. Like so many Russian stations this resembles a run-down palace. We have a short walk across Karl Marx Square to the school of the same name. It's an imposing building, built in 1902—but it's firmly locked.

The teacher Alexei goes away to phone, but can't raise the janitor who has been seeing in the New Year too well. It is, after all, only 3 January.

We freeze as we wait. Eventually two senior girls from the school appear. They show us that entry is possible through a window round the back. We all squeeze our frozen bodies and our bags into the building which is to be our home for the next five days and find the gym hall where we've been told to put our mattresses.

The kids who, individually, are charming, are noisy, selfish and wild as a group. They swarm up ropes and bars, but eventually come to our aid with the luggage. There's nowhere to sit: just low benches around the gym, where the kids are screaming away.

The two mothers start preparing soup and macaroni on two electric rings they've brought with them in their luggage, but which we now discover don't work properly. The macaroni doesn't cook, but burns. Since it's now very late, we decide to leave the macaroni till later and have a combined lunch and breakfast of soup, bread, butter (a luxury which after today will be served only with buckwheat porridge) and slices of cheese.

The police appear. We've been seen climbing through the window and have been reported. They take some persuading, but eventually are satisfied we're genuine and go away.

The corridor which runs at right angles from the gym hall past the dining-room is warm. The mothers decide we'll put the mattresses there at night. We eat soup and wash up in sinks along the corridor. The water is cold and there's no soap. We look round the town. It's down-at-heel, but former splendours are still visible. Churches gleam gold against the frosty sky, and we enter the Monastery of the Transfiguration of the Saviour—forcibly closed at the Revolution—with fading frescoes in the porchway. There are two gates; the main gates, through which we enter the fourteenth-century kremlin area of this ancient town, and little low doors at the side. The small gates represented the door to paradise, the big gates the way to hell.

Heaven and hell: the contrasts sum up this country of paradox, and perhaps to live here is to be in purgatory...

It's too late to do any sightseeing today, so we head out for the park. It's good to be out in the crisp air. People are skiing and sledging. Our kids join in, sliding downhill on their bottoms; sitting on the ice, arms round each other; collapsing with yells of pleasure. I'm glad their mothers can't see, especially the mother of the girl wearing a quilted coat.

We see the domes of closed churches, splendid against the fading light of the frosty sky. So much has been abandoned, laid waste, lost. I ask Nadia, the musicologist, what might have happened if Russia had had no revolution—no network of streets named Lenin Avenue, October Avenue, Freedom Street, The Street of the Bolshevik October, and, inevitably, Tereshkova Street... She replies that her grandparents would never have been educated. They were Jewish and were forced to live in a restricted area outside St Petersburg.

We get our first glimpse of the frozen Volga. Dark shapes on the ice are fishermen. Boats are grounded. The frozen river is stilled.

Shops are open. The mothers hunt for cheese. Yaroslavl is famed for its cheese, and friends in St Petersburg have asked them to bring some back. But although Yaroslavl cheesemakers have won prizes in cheese-making competitions open to all the former socialist countries there's none in any of the shops. A shop assistant mops muddy puddles of melted snow from hundreds of trampling feet. She's using a dirty cloth. I try to think what it must be like to know no other world, no other way of shopping, no other life...

We pass the large Church of the Epiphany with its traditional five pale blue domes representing Christ and the four evangelists. Built at the end of the seventeenth century, it's richly decorated with broad bands of white and green tiles.

But as we cross the road home we see, standing on its own, very small and compact, another red-walled church, which is still used for worship. It's just the size of a small chapel, warm, festive and very welcoming. Candles burn on a stand. Some of our children buy candles from two very young girls, a nun and a novice, and add their light to the bright little flames.

I buy a book about the lives of noteworthy nuns up to the Revolution. I read it that evening after supper, sitting huddled against a radiator while the kids play a noisy game with Alexei in the gym hall, and the two mothers—Valentina and Lidia—cook for the next day. I feel isolated and foreign.

Bed is what I'd like. A long hot soak in a bath. I marvel at the stamina of the other women. The mothers brew tea. I slice bread. It's supper time. A large brown cockroach crawls across the corridor where I've been sitting and where we were planning to sleep. Lidia squashes it with her foot. We shudder. It's to be the gym hall for us, cold or not.

In fact, with a coat over my sleeping-bag I'm warm. But the kids who haven't brought sleeping-bags wake up frozen, so I part with my coat.

The mothers waken horrified. They heard a rat gnawing in the wall behind us in the night.

I waken aching, trying not to think of what it's like to sleep in a proper bed.

We breakfast off porridge the mothers have cooked the night before, milky corn coffee, bread which is already going dry and cheese. Then we trudge through the snow to the trolleybus stop to go back to the station, this time for a trip to Rostov Vieliki (great Rostov), another old town with a church complex and two monasteries, both 'working', as Russians say for a church in use.

We get into a local train with wooden seats. A man complains, 'You shouldn't be here: it's a workman's coach.' I can't see any difference between this and any other coach, and the man himself looks as though he's been on a pension for years. It fills up with other old comrades, one of whom starts to sing, to the delight of our kids who clap wholeheartedly.

I sit squashed up with the other adults of our party. They're all quick speakers, except for Valentina, a woman of character, blonde bobbed hair, slim and smart, in jeans, a white hat, a pink jacket—a single parent aware of her place in the St Petersburg intelligentsia. She is a chemist, I learn, and did all her training in French, to be sent to one of the former French colonies in Africa—but it never worked out. 'I'm glad,' says Zhenya, her daughter, feelingly. 'I wouldn't have liked to have lived there.' Zhenya is an admirable child, sweet, obedient, a poet.

We're soon in the country. Little can be seen through the filthy double-glazed windows. I make out wooden houses, some boarded up—obviously used only in the summer—others lived in, forests, and here and there the gold dome of a church crowns the sky.

We arrive at the station of Rostov Vieliki. I'm the butt of good humour as we queue for the ladies' loo which I enter squeamishly. It's one of the crouch-over variety with no flush facilities. But it's clean—and it has a door (unlike the ones in the school).

The women rush off to shop for cheese. I find enamel bowls and mugs for sale among foodstuffs. As I've brought no crockery with me, I buy these necessities, which I then have to carry for the rest of the day.

So this is my introduction to one of the loveliest of all Russia's small historic towns. Even in the grey, below-zero January weather I fall in love with Rostov, which was once a major trading centre, standing as it does on the banks of a large lake, with access to tributaries of the Volga.

We head for the centre of the town, walking up a street of small wooden houses, many boarded up, sadly neglected; no amenities—but beautifully carved shutters, once the pride and joy of a provident householder. I recall Turgenev's descriptions of peasant houses and imagine small-town life a hundred years ago.

Some of the larger houses, once the homes of prosperous merchants, have painted rosettes decorating the walls.

We visit the famous kremlin. Built in the seventeenth century, it immediately became one of the wonders of Old Russia. It covers a large area with a spacious courtyard and beautiful buildings.

Unusually for Russia, it contains no cathedral. The limestone walls and five green domes of the Cathedral of the Dormition are adjacent to the kremlin, linking the Cathedral to both the kremlin itself and the town, with its arched shopping centre and the Church of the Saviour of the Market.

The kremlin walls and towers were built in 1670. Five separate churches were incorporated into the structure of beautifully patterned limestone walls. The Church of the Resurrection, and the Church of St John the Divine stand beside the entrance gates, supported by graceful round towers.

Ceremonial processions passed in and out of these, and the Holy Gates and the churches were covered with frescoes of rare beauty. This is an art which requires great skill, as the paint is applied straight to the plaster.

We are not able to see inside the churches, partly because of the time of year and partly because restoration work is being carried on.

We walk around spacious courtyards and look up at golden domes shining splendidly in the winter sunlight. It's freezing but the kids stand respectfully listening to the guide who leads us past guest houses where church and civic dignitaries (including the Russian royal family) have stayed, and on through a low narrow gateway to the frozen lake where the domes of a monastery are visible to our right. Men are fishing on the lake where they've bored holes into the ice.

The Rostov kremlin boasts the largest bell tower and the heaviest bell in all Europe: thirty-five tonnes I think our guide said. The thirteen bells which rang from the mighty four-tiered tower have been part of the life of peasant and noble, soldier and bride, chiming for weddings and for prayer; welcoming soldiers home from the battlefield; sounding in solemn funerals for the souls of the departed; giving warning of fire or war. And now they are being rung for services once again.

We go into the museum, once the Metropolitan's house. We're glad to defrost. There's an impressive exhibition of beautiful local painted enamelwork: modern jewellery; glowing miniatures, flowers, landscapes, Russian fairy tales; portraits; lockets. This miniature work, used nowadays for jewellery, is known as *finift* in Russian. Traditionally, the colours are pale pink and blue.

The exhibition is of enormous interest, showing not only the craftsmanship of the Rostov enamellers, but Russian social life through the last three centuries.

I happen to start my survey at the most modern part and so I work my way back. There are delicate flowers for all seasons of the year, lovely small landscapes, lake scenes, birches, miniature paintings of Russian folksongs and fairy tales. There are portraits including, inevitably, the poet Pushkin. There is a portrait of Lenin and even one of Stalin.

And now I'm in the nineteenth century. There are small icons, sorrowful Madonnas. As I go back in time the secular themes are replaced by religious ones. There is a whole series on the Stations of the Cross; Christ scourged in miniature. Ornate ancient chalices, the crowns of clergy, crosses—all are adorned with this exquisite miniature work.

Down wooden stairs, in the low, single-columned White Chamber, we visit another exhibition. Church art, I suppose we'd call it: but these fourteenth and fifteenth-century icons are too powerful to be 'art', too sacred for a museum. I notice a superbly carved fifteenth-century limestone cross, and other smaller things. I think what wealth was vandalized by invading armies, of the excesses of anti-religious revolutionaries in 1917.

There's a room devoted to the fourteenth-century St Sergius of Radonezh. I look at engravings from a nineteenth-century book of the saint's life in which its original owner has left his own pencilled notes. A prince kneels, receives the holy man's blessing. Power which owns a higher source: Russia lost that in the blasphemy of men who made themselves gods. Here in Rostov I'm seeing the heart of a Russia which is not just historic but holy.

After the museum, Valentina, Zhenia and I go to the museum shop.

But we lose our group. We set out in the direction we saw them heading for, but find only the frozen lake, the fishermen and the towers of the monastery across the way.

Now begins a trudge of many hours round and round the kremlin walls investigating every possible eating-place in the hope of finding our group. My boots are too big and heavy. The lining of my coat clings to my legs.

It's well after 2p.m. and we've eaten and drunk nothing since 7.30a.m. We find a canteen, eat goulash, a slice of bread, drink sugared tea, give up all hope of finding the group and head for the station. We board an electric train, then decide, as it's only three o'clock, that we may as well go back and see the monastery. We jump off the train—just in time. Its doors slide shut and it leaves. Then we discover it wasn't even the Yaroslavl train!

Twelve-year-old Zhenya who has uncomplainingly shared the fruitless trudge in quest of our group, laughs. 'Another adventure,' she decides.

It's a forty-minute walk to the monastery, past decorated wooden houses, most of them now sadly run down. One has 'post letters here' in pre-Revolutionary script. We go into an area of newer houses, all of five storeys; the number of floors was planned so that there wouldn't need to be a lift. We have a quick look in another shop—but there's no cheese.

As we go towards the monastery in the dusk, the Rostov bells ring. We hear them chime out, a joyous major key. We've been told the ringers stand so that they can see one another and keep in time—and that the chimes can be heard up to twenty kilometres away. It's fine to hear the bells ringing out at the end of the brief January day—almost like a special word from the town to us, from the heart of Russia itself.

The monastery is right on the shores of the lake, where the fishermen are packing up now after their day on the ice.

The monks were ejected at the Revolution. Many, many of the religious—nuns and monks—perished in the ice of the Gulag. Starved and dying, many of them were able to bring spiritual help to other prisoners, prophetic words of encouragement and hope.

Religious life, the life of a monk especially, so totally

contradicted Soviet 'reality' that it wasn't really supposed to exist. But it's such a vital part of Orthodoxy that it has never died out and now monasteries like this one of St Jacob in Rostov are being reopened. Buildings which once housed guest rooms, monks' cells, libraries, stand within the monastery walls, as well as two churches, one built by two serf architects who belonged to a wealthy count. We see its closed doors, its dark windows. But there are lights in the windows of the other church and we enter in time to catch the beginning of evening prayer, led by a novice and a layman in shabby jersey and faded jeans, his hair drawn back into a pony-tail.

It's very poignant: the dim lights, dilapidated walls, candlelight, prayers. We don't stay long, however. Belief for Valentina means you visit famous churches (she can reel off quite a list of them) and light a candle. I ask her if she understands the chanted prayers. She says, no: but the liturgy isn't meant for the untutored, it's not like the sermon, which everyone should be able to understand.

I buy an icon of St Seraphim of Sarov. Two young novices in black cassocks serve me. 'All icons here are blessed,' they say. I tell them, 'This is for a priest in Scotland.' 'Is he Orthodox?' they ask, and put the icon down. I fear they won't give blessed Orthodox saints into heretic hands, but they get another and put the display one back in its place.

It's dark outside. A local granny with a little boy follows us out of the church.

A bus! We muster our energy and run for it. It's already filling up with fishermen and their sons, all heading like us for the electric train. Valentina tells me the Russian name for the drills they carry to bore the ice, tells me how her father used to take her fishing on the frozen waters of the lakes around Leningrad...

At the station we find our missing group. Back at base we wash dishes. Our children are disobedient. When we ask them to help, they pull faces, argue. And with a trickle of lukewarm water, no soap, it's easier to do it ourselves.

Next day is a local trip, thank goodness. We get shown round the Monastery of the Transfiguration in Yaroslavl. Our guide is small and plump and pleasant, with round glasses beneath her round fur hat. She's good at talking to children. She speaks positively about monastic life, though she points out that the rich and powerful took the tonsure at the end of their lives as a way of winning salvation. Having been on top in this life they didn't want to miss out in the next, and the teaching was that the only thing purer than a monk is a newborn child.

When restoration work was carried out, the guide tells us, they found bones of monks which glowed with holiness. The monastery ground itself was supposed to pulse with blessing. Is any of that power left today to bless and heal this stricken land, I wonder?

The air is crisp and cold—eighteen degrees below. We're glad to go into the warmth of a museum displaying early manuscripts. Rich *boyars* (nobles) made handsome donations over the years and the monastery was found to possess thousands of rare books, including over a thousand volumes of Greek manuscripts. At the end of the eighteenth century a twelfth-century manuscript of *The Lay of Prince Igor's Host* was discovered. Until very recently that unique manuscript was on display, but some visiting archivists voiced their concern at seeing such a precious, irreplaceable manuscript kept on public display. So artists made very careful copies and this is what we are now seeing.

As well as *The Lay*, we look at copies of the earliest Russian writing on pieces of birch bark, the first Gospel, the first manuscripts. We trace Russian history in manuscript from its earliest days through the Tatar-Mongol invasions into the present day. But pride of place is given to *The Lay* which was translated into something like twenty-nine languages.

On display too is a 1970s letter from Leeds about a performance of Borodin's opera *Prince Igor*, in which the actor playing the Mongol emperor had broken both arms. Photographs on display showed how costumes were draped to hide the plaster.

The mothers and I leave the children playing in the snow with teacher Alexei and walk into town where we drink hot sweet coffee and eat bread and cheese in a dark café dominated by a television playing Western rock music and showing a steamy near-nude show.

We set out for the shops once more in a vain quest for the famous Yaroslavl cheese, but none is to be found. I understand now why Russians walk slowly: the weariness of life, heavy footwear, and the need to keep your feet planted firmly on icy pavements have bred this slow gait.

Churches stand on every corner of the town centre: in use and abandoned. The town's emblem of the bear with a sickle gleams above frozen snow.

The children return. They generously give me packs of postcards they've bought, show me their books. Zhenya, model child as ever, has bought a copy of *The Lay of Prince Igor's Host.*

After lunch, Valentina, Zhenya and I seek cleanliness. We opt for the local hotel. The guard on duty, with his red armband, can't guarantee that the floor ladies will allow outsiders like us to use the washing facilities. But he's not at all officious and lets us in. We try every floor and on the fourth are successfully admitted to a shower. We enjoy the hot water. Valentina and Zhenya tell me to use the shower first and then ask, 'Why didn't you stay longer?' I dry Zhenya's back; we share shampoo, talcum powder.

Washing is a serious business in Russia. We go home to the greeting, 'With light steam.' Which is what you have to say when someone comes out of a bath.

And so to bed ... for tomorrow is Orthodox Christmas Eve.

20

Russian Christmas

On 6 January we get up at 6a.m. for a train which takes three hours to travel eighty kilometres to Kostroma, an industrial town with some rare wooden churches, a kremlin, museums at its heart. It's Christmas Eve, and to pass the time on the long, slow train journey we practise carols which we will sing tonight at our Christmas celebration.

The train fills with country people. The faces of the women bear witness to their hard lives; the men bear the marks of heavy drinking.

'A restricted life,' Valentina offers, 'but they're good people.' And she tells me how, when she was a student and wandered around Russia, country people would take her in and give her a bed.

'In fact,' she said, 'I can't understand how in the Christmas story the innkeeper says there's no room. That wouldn't happen in Russia. A peasant family would never turn people away, especially not a pregnant woman. They'd sleep in the barn themselves. The baby would be wrapped up and put beside the stove.'

I'm sure this is true. People who live so close to earth, in such bitter winters, know full well the value of life ...

They know too how to endure. We stiffen, sitting on hard seats, and are glad to empty out onto a snowbound platform. Everyone heads for a tumbledown building. Some of the girls and

I decline. It's all too obvious from the outside what the inside will be like. And the looks on our children's faces as they come out... 'Just the same,' says Zhenya, piteously, 'I can't last out. Come with me, Mum.'

We hurtle across the icy road and crowd into a small café with a counter and two tables. We stand around the tables and revive with freshly baked buns, and warm liquid which passes as coffee.

Our neighbour, who's drinking a big jar of what I guess is *kvass*, a kind of very low-alcohol beer made by souring bread and adding liquid, shares slices of his own salted pig fat and bread with us. He's probably still in his fifties, on an army pension. Intelligent blue eyes, ruddy face, a blond beard filled with grey, the inevitable fur hat. When he hears I come from Scotland he tells me he's been reading Walter Scott.

A horse pulls a cart across the frozen square. We catch a trolleybus to the town centre where we find a jolly scene. For the first time in seventy years Christmas is a public holiday. This year it's an economic necessity. Factories have closed for lack of materials; it's cheaper to give everyone a holiday.

There are coloured lights on fir trees, the sounds of bells and ponies giving rides. Actors with loudspeakers are out on the square, and crowds gather to watch their old folk tales: Baba Jaga, the witch, a friendly bear, a couple of pirates. The age-old tradition of guisers, mummers... I'm glad to see it revived, and enjoy watching the crowd watching the actors.

Our children rush off to buy chocolate ices. Breathing the frozen air is ice-cream enough for me. And indeed they're soon complaining of cold.

We catch a bus and then walk along Socialist Street between wooden houses and wooden churches. I glimpse the golden domes of a monastery framed by the graceful frosty branches of birches.

An elderly lady with three small boys joins us, asks the way. She has come with her grandsons from another town to find a church.

Two tourist buses are parked outside the gates of the monastery-museum. A pensioner is selling rosebuds carved from birch bark. We buy some.

'I could make them too, I'm sure,' says Zhenya, 'but I'm sorry for the birches.'

I'm sorry for the man too, standing for hours in the snow.

We go into a museum church covered from floor to ceiling with glowing frescoes taking us through the festivals of the church into heaven, where God the Father holds the Son, and the Spirit hovers in dove-like form. There's an open-air museum of wooden churches, too, but they're all closed for the winter. The children run around them, climb steps to locked doors.

Tsar Mikhail, the first of the Romanov line, hid here from Poles in the seventeenth century and the house he stayed in is now a museum of peasant life. There are quotes from the wisdom of Lenin painted round the walls, richly embroidered dresses, basketwork shoes and furniture, ornately carved distaffs—and whips and canes used to punish serfs.

The place shuts at three o'clock for the holiday, and it's already getting dark as we walk across a frozen river—the first time in my life I've ever walked on solid ice. It's a tributary of the Volga. We see huge blocks of ice sticking out of the frozen water. Our eyes absorb a white, snowbound world. Behind us are the towers and domes of the past: ahead factory chimneys, smoke, an industrial town.

We trudge into its heart. Steam rises from manholes in the road, caught by the headlights of battered trucks. We pass hideous housing blocks, dilapidated wooden houses with carved shutters.

We find a canteen. Good thick home-made soup is followed by the inevitable buckwheat *kasha* to which the mothers have added our own tinned meat. We drink compote—hot water poured over dried raisins and prunes.

A senile soul is sitting at the table beside us with a pile of dry bread and a glass of tea. A little shamefacedly we pass her our leftovers, but she receives them without demur and later we see her eating the scrapings from other plates.

Fortified, we slither over pavements again, to hear the sound of little bells, singing. A young couple in white robes comes towards us. The girl wears a veil, the man a cap like a novice's with a red cross marked on it. They sing as they walk: 'Glory to you, O Lord, glory to you. Glory to you, Mother of God, glory to you.'

I assume they're Orthodox. Later I'm told they belong to a sect called 'The Whites' because of the white robes they wear. They have weird ideas, turning the Mother of God into a white-robed goddess. They have turned young people against their parents and, in Moscow at any rate, have been banned from the main metro stations. In St Petersburg they preach quite openly and never fail to draw an attentive crowd. (However, by the following autumn they became completely discredited when they wrongly predicted the end of the world.)

In the shops women greet each other: 'With the festival.'

It's a festival which hasn't been kept for more than seventy years. We shall celebrate this evening, but unfortunately we have a long wait in the station. The buffet sells apples, which I share with the children. We've had no fruit all week. Alexei eats Georgian savouries, which look interesting. I buy a newspaper called *We*, an American-Russian production, that shows the glossy life of the West, and reflect that there are values to be lost as well as gained...

The journey home takes three and a half hours. It's after 10p.m. and we're all shattered. I'd like to go to bed, but we still have our Christmas celebrations. The meal consists of stale bread and tinned meat. But we set the table with candles and add sweets. A child has brought a box of chocolates. I have small packets of Mars bars, knowing that the children see these things advertised on television. They're on sale in the booths but at prices ordinary families can't afford, so it makes them feel that they've been given a treat.

Then we sing carols and suddenly it all comes together, as the pure sounds of 'Silent Night' fill the dingy school dining-room, Nadia's voice ringing out like a bell. The children read the Christmas story from the Gospels, and we play what Valentina assures us are traditional games, making shapes with candlewax and water, and a big mess to be cleaned up later.

We move out into the hall, playing a game in and under arches made by holding up our arms. They all want to do this ceaselessly. I opt out eventually, wash dishes and crash out about 2.30a.m. (we've been up since six!). The mothers go to our 'fridge' (the double panes of the gym hall)—and discover that we were burgled while we were keeping Christmas. Small packets of processed cheese have gone. So have the choicest of our remaining foodstuffs, including a packet of digestive biscuits which cost over £3.50 in the currency shop.

What a good thing, we agree, that we weren't able to buy supplies of the expensive Yaroslavl cheese—that would have been stolen too.

We sleep late on Christmas morning. Valentina is always the first up. I follow her into the dining-room and we find a newly broken pane of glass. Someone has obviously been trying to get in: Valentina said she saw a powerfully-built young man move away as she switched the light on. We recall our easy entrance from a ground-floor window and feel very glad that tonight we'll be safely on a train.

Feeling very untrusting, I take my personal stereo and my gas-operated curling brush with me. I'm ashamed to say too that I had specially bought an aerosol can of perfumed deodorant in St Petersburg, and I use this liberally. I realize it's my personal protest against the dirt around us—like the Elizabethans, sniffing cloves and oranges!

We catch a trolley to a vast grove of birch trees at the edge of the Volga. People are cross-country skiing; whole families are out sledging. It's Christmas Day. We're heading for a monastery looked after by nuns across the Volga, but we already know we're too late for the morning service.

We walk across the great River Volga; an experience, again, for me, to be walking across a wide expanse of frozen river water, to be walking across this particular river... We clamber up the frozen bank, entering the monastery through an archway of faded, destroyed frescoes. The Lord looks tenderly down at us. The multitude of heaven greets us, haloes gleaming gold—it's easy to imagine the rich sight this was once. As we come out under the arch we look back. Above our heads gleam newly-restored icons. There are more on on the church wall facing us.

A very young nun with a goat's-wool shawl over her black robe, passes us. We ask the way to Mother Superior. She doesn't raise her eyes as she talks to us.

The snow is falling thickly as Valentina (who is counting on a foreign visitor for grace from Mother Superior) and I go to the nun's quarters and find Mother Superior, a statuesque woman wearing a high headdress, a jewelled cross on her breast. She promises us an escort. We wait outside. Some of our girls come, wanting a blessing. Valentina tells them to go and ask, but they are chased away. Our guide comes out. She's a nun in her mid-thirties, perhaps; high cheekbones, a pleasant face. She wears glasses. An edging of dark hair parted in the middle shows under her veil. A shawl over her long black coat is her only protection from the weather. She tells us how she came here to find it all in ruins—and soon shows us an unrestored church. 'It was all like this,' she says. 'I felt quite alarmed. I didn't think it was possible to live here. There were only seven of us then. We worked day and night, but with God's help...'

She is holding black gloves in her hands. She's an artist, an icon painter, but here you do whatever you're told to do, you make no plans of your own. We see slips of girls, novices in black headscarves and dresses, cleaning the church floor after the Christmas Day service.

She talks about the monastery. Like so many, it was destroyed by the Poles, rebuilt, to be destroyed again by the Bolsheviks. The cemetery was axed, crosses hewn. Only a few sad-looking stones, without any crosses, stand now amongst the snow.

One hundred and twenty women live here—from Latvia and the Ukraine, from St Petersburg and Vladivostok. Their ages range from a girl of fifteen to women in their seventies.

Local people attach themselves to our group, listen curiously, ask questions. We go into a snowbound garden. Ancient cedars grow here and in summer (I think at the Feast of Pentecost) nuns offer visitors the fallen cones.

The nuns get up at 5 each day. They have ten cows which have to be milked before morning prayer. They're self supporting, gathering the inevitable berries and mushrooms, scything hay. Visitors come, some just to look, others to stay, and they help with some of the chores. Morning prayer lasts from six til nine. and only then do they have breakfast. Then come the jobs for the day, lunch, more work, and evening prayer from five until eight, with supper to follow. Someone asks about holidays: they get one week, once a year, except those who come from Vladivostok who are given extra time to allow for travel.

'Suppose you want to leave?' a woman wonders. 'Do people run away?'

Some do, we're told; and two asked to leave and received permission. 'But,' says our 'little mother', 'they weren't happy. You leave one cross behind only to find another, more heavy to bear.'

The snow is falling thickly now. Two of the men who have joined our group, local townspeople in their forties or fifties, stand bareheaded.

'From the way you speak I can tell you've had an education,' one woman says, and she sounds surprised, because she has been brought up to feel herself less educated than people in Moscow and St Petersburg and to think that people with an education would never choose a simple, even primitive way of life, would not choose to believe in God.

'Here you accept everything,' the nun says, serenely. 'That's monasticism: suffering, reconciliation, obedience. If you think someone's wronged you, you must forgive. If you're told to do something and you've planned to do something else, you say, "I accept".'

We listen in silence. It is Christmas Day. Valentina asks the nun for advice for our children.

'Believe, go to church, live a Christian way, save your soul,' the nun says. 'Above all, love God. That's what I want for you. That you love the Lord.'

Then we go back into the church, empty now after the service, where the children light candles, buy small icons, cards. We walk back across the Volga, looking behind us to the monastery, whose golden domes rise from the bank of the river, drawing townspeople and pilgrims.

This is a fitting end to our memorable stay. We leave on the night train and go back to the Karl Marx school to cook and pack. Some of the children come with us; others stay to slide on their bottoms down icy slopes.

We tidy the rooms and then sit on hard chairs without any backs in the school dining-room, our luggage piled about us—and Lidia and Nadia start to sing. They sing folk songs in harmony, their voices rising and falling through verse after verse. They serenade Valentina and me with 'The Volga boatmen'. Lidia laughs over one of the verses of the song, in which the boatmen who toil along the river bank roped to the barges like mules supposedly say: 'The English are wise—they use machines.' These women have never seen an automatic washing-machine. Lidia works in a factory, hasn't washed all week. She's toiled in the kitchen, coping with the feeble electric rings. Her rich contralto rings out. Harmony dances in our dingy surroundings. This is a nation of song.

Lidia tells me she didn't have her voice trained because her mother developed cancer and Lidia stayed at home to look after her. She and her father nursed her day and night—with no pain control.

Then we catch the night train home to St Petersburg. I stretch out, switch on my personal stereo—and Dvorak's cello concerto takes me into a world as mysterious and lovely as the landscapes and frescoes, the golden-domed churches, the majestic chimes of the Rostov bells: the heart of Old Russia which I have just heard and seen.

21

Division—and the Touch of a Hovering Wing

As we step off the train in St Petersburg after our journey to historic Russia mothers come to meet our school party. One of them tells me, triumphantly, 'It's over, they've split.'

'What?' I can't believe her words.

'They've split,' she tells me. 'We're taking our children away.'

I hurry home to find Stuart. He's looking drawn and tired. So-called peace talks have been going on day and night and into the small hours, and he's had a full programme teaching the Finnish Lutheran deacons' courses too.

'So what's this about a split?' I say.

'The Society is going to split,' he explains. 'The students in the Institute have already gone, but the school's not going to be affected, not until the end of May. Then the sixth class will be divided and we'll lose the tenth class too. They all signed an agreement.'

'So why are the mothers all saying they're taking the children away?'

'Because they are,' he explains, 'but not until May.'

How wrong can you be!

That evening there's a meeting of staff and parents. In a last-minute bid to save the Society, Sonia offers to chair it—as a neutral person. And she puts me up beside her. The group is plainly divided into two camps. The former members of the Society who discussed philosophy endlessly have all opted out.

The Society as we knew it, the Society Stuart and I came here to join, is over. Only Boris and Lena and one or two friends of theirs are left.

So what about the school? This is what the meeting is to decide.

Stuart and I are dumbfounded. Had he not sat up till three o'clock two nights in a row, until they'd managed to sign an agreement saying, as he told me, that no changes would be made to the school. What more could there be to discuss?

To our dismay we realize that even the peace talks, even the signed agreement, haven't been able to hold the school together. So bitter are the feelings between the two groups—Boris and Lena and the teacher Alexei who took the children away on our trip on the one hand, and the deputy head and his side on the other—that they are determined to split the school. Despite Sonia's moderating influence the meeting is bloody. People hurl insults across the table. Lena keeps trying to reply but Boris restrains her. And Alexei, who is hearing terrible accusations about himself, keeps silent too.

A woman speaks up. 'I'm not a parent, but I've come to represent my godson.'

I nod. I know the boy. He started in the sixth class midway through the autumn term. He's not, I think, as academically able as some of the other children, but he has a gentle nature. I noticed that when he was chosen to take the part of Joseph in the nativity play he did so with absolute solemnity and I could see how much it meant to him.

'His mother's an invalid,' this woman went on. 'He hasn't got a dad at home. He thinks the world of Alexei Andreevich.'

Sonia nods too. But I look at the people gathered round the table. Their faces are stony. And I know that because this woman isn't an intellectual, because she's just an ordinary person, her words don't carry any weight. It has all boiled down to a few people thinking that their children are better, more cultured, more intelligent than others. I feel anguish about this whole situation boiling inside me.

'You can't divide children like this...' I protest. And I plead, 'Give the school a chance. We've been struggling with nothing: no textbooks, no blackboards.'

But the faces around me remain stony. I feel the way people must have done in the old Communist days when they were being defrocked by their Party cadre and found no one to support them. 'You're committing a crime against children!' I say hotly, and feel tears welling into my eyes.

In the end, parents, teachers are put to a public confession: 'My child is staying; my child is going. I'm going; I'm staying.'

'I only know one school,' Sonia says, when her turn comes.

So, it has happened. All Sonia's prayers, the work she put into the nativity play, Stuart's peace talks, the papers he drew up... all to no avail. And our school trip... Two boys who have sat side by side like David and Jonathan for two-and-a-half years, who were never apart in all those hours we were away together on our trip, are split up: one will attend the breakaway group, the other will stay in our dismembered school. Zhenya, whose back I dried, is split away too.

The eighth class is safe, but only because there's no suitable building.

There's no building for the tenth class or half of the sixth class, at first, either and for three or four weeks children who have been close friends meet in two different wings of the same building, share the same canteen, but sit apart at lessons. During the intervals a few brave souls try to join their sundered friends, until in the end the new sixth class is taken off to another building and we never see them again.

Bloody battles continue. What we're living with now is a situation like a divorce. Both sides are now fighting over maintenance—not this time of children, but of textbooks, blackboards. There are terrible scenes in which locks are burst, people accuse one another of stealing...

Out of this comes, amazingly, the thing I've been wanting ever since coming here: a full programme of Bible teaching with the eighth class and the truncated sixth. Sonia helps me, giving me every support, both with the content of the lessons and the language.

And we have a visitor from England, bringing news from home, Christmas cards, packets of food.

One evening midweek, we catch the end of evening prayer in the Vladimir Church. They are singing carols. The melodies float around the building. People crowd closer. The Metropolitan is present. He stands, blesses us, speaks. His voice is old and shaky. He is virtually carried along in a procession through our midst, to stand at the doors of the church where he speaks again. I can't make out what he said but Stuart tells me afterwards he has, typically, told everyone to remain true to the teachings of Orthodoxy. The old priest bows. People say, 'thank you,' return the bows. Their faces are smiling and relaxed as they leave.

A woman comes towards us. 'Wasn't that wonderful,' she says, 'wasn't it wonderful?' Her lined face is shining. 'Wonderful,' she repeats. Her face is bathed with happiness. It is unearthly, this joy. She kisses me, turns to Stuart, to our friend. 'I am a holy woman,' she says. 'Let me kiss your forehead.' She's very small. Stuart bends low to receive her kiss. Our visitor from England receives the kiss of the holy woman too.

After all the trauma Stuart goes away to Finland for a break. I don't want to go: I have my Bible teaching to do, and, anyway, I'd rather stay in Russia. Two weeks away would be very bad for my language, I argue.

So I head for a bath. And I listen to music: Gorecki's Third Symphony, an unexpected Christmas present from friends who knew exactly what to choose. It's sung in Polish, which provides a switch-off point for me—a sort of rebellion against Russian (despite my earlier protests), which I revel in all on my own.

However, I'm never good on my own. Night-time, locking up time, is always the worst. I try not to think of those dark empty corridors, rooms opening off from me—nor to think of anyone who might have sneaked in earlier and be lurking there.

So, midweek, I spend the night away with Nina, a friend who speaks near-perfect English and has lived in England, in America, in India. She shows me photographs of Mother Teresa. 'Look,' she says. 'That's my boss—he was building an electric dam in India and I was his interpreter. Look how he's posing, and look at Mother Teresa, standing there, so simply.'

Nina said that after meeting Mother Teresa her boss looked 'like a real human being' for the next twenty-four hours. For herself it was a turning-point, a source of spiritual strength. Meeting Mother Teresa had been, for Nina, like receiving a holy woman's kiss.

Anastasia, who has come with us, had her meeting with her own 'holy woman' too. Anastasia is a gentle person, with beautiful black hair, pink-rimmed glasses, tiny hands, tiny voice. For her the 'holy woman' was an elderly Englishwoman she met long ago in the sixties. Her senior asked her to translate for this woman. 'I can't,' Anastasia blurted out, 'you know we're not allowed to talk to foreigners.'

But assured of her senior's permission, Anastasia acted as an interpreter for the elderly English lady. She said it was like meeting a being from another world. Her new friend had said to her, 'You're different from the others. They only say what they want me to hear—you tell the truth.' They met again the next year, and the lady asked, 'What can I bring you from England?' 'A Bible,' Anastasia answered. And so she received her first ever Bible.

She talked about her last meeting with her friend—in the Moscow Hotel. They covered the telephone with pillows. 'I shan't come here again,' the English woman said. 'I know you believe. Let me baptize you.'

But Anastasia was frightened. 'I know nothing... This isn't for me...'

The elderly lady took off her cross and fastened it around Anastasia's neck. Anastasia wore it secretly—in memory of her friend, who died very soon afterwards.

Nina is worried about Anastasia who has invested so many hopes in our Society and feels hurt and upset by the split. We talk about the troubles of our Society and agree that they mirror the problems of Russia as a whole. 'People are wounded,' Nina and Anastasia say, 'after seventy years of totalitarianism. Russia is sick.'

Nina's husband works in the docks built by Peter the Great: there's no work now for him. Some men come only to drink all day; others come hung-over from the night before. Only three or four of them, like himself, want to work; but there's nothing to do. He showed me brass hooks and handles and rails he's made at work for their *dacha*.

'I'm a farmer now,' he said, and explained that they have a large piece of land, several acres, worked by a tractor. Everything has to be carried. They get the electric train and afterwards they have to walk. There are no roads. The nearest village has only a few very elderly people. In the summer it teems with life: all the relatives of people who used to live there come back.

Owning their own plot of land, growing their own vegetables is how people survive. It's also a protest against the drab uniformity of everyday life, the exploitation and ruination of the countryside under collectivization.

We eat mushroom soup—they've gathered the mushrooms themselves—and salad made with their own beetroots and potatoes. Later Nina gives me a jar of berries they've picked and preserved in layers of sugar.

I see a copy of *Walden* on her table. Thoreau would have approved of the way she and her husband work the land. Not only the land: their flat is spotless, with glass doors and mirrors making it seem bigger. They've done it all themselves.

I think about the injury in people's minds, relationships, understanding of life, as I catch the electric train back to town. There's a crush, so I stand by the doors. At one station the doors open and I see that the part of the platform in front of my coach has completely broken away—so if anyone from my coach had wanted to leave the train, they would have had problems.

Sonia's husband, Sasha, tells me Communism was like two great pincers which tore deeply into the lives of everyone. Sasha was hurt too. He voted against Communistic proposals in his medical section in the Red Army—and paid a price. Because he'd raised his head, he got noted and because of that he got put on duty every New Year, stayed in hostels and communal flats when others got better housing—and was posted to Afghanistan...

I listen to him speak. His grandfather was a Cossack. The heritage of the steppes runs in his veins. They put him on a horse when he was only three. There was no church, but there were icons, kept hidden in a drawer. Although Easter is not a holiday, the family continued to eat *kulich*, the traditional Easter cake.

'My mother said, "God bless this work," when she went out to dig potatoes. She said, "Glory to thee, O Lord." I didn't know it was a prayer,' Sasha says, and as he speaks I think of the faith that they could not wipe out, the wounds deep in this man's psyche, this disturbing story of the pincers of Communism, the tentacles of evil. I remember how someone said on my first visit here, 'This is the land of Mordor.'

How much this troubled land needs a holy, healing touch! Sasha's own father was orphaned when he was only six. It was in the thirties, when Stalin's resettlement programmes were causing starvation and distress on a massive scale. The little boy was simply left to wander, starving and alone. He made good. But, when he lay dying, his last cry was for the mother he had lost when he was hungry, alone and frightened all those years before. How deep the hunger, how unhealed the hurt.

Sonia says, suddenly: 'What will heal a human heart?'

And do I not need the healing touch as much as anyone? I am so impoverished, the Russian language heavy on my tongue, denying myself the freedom to think deeply in my own, quite literally tongue-tied. I turn from the face of Christ every day in the beggar woman on her knees holding out her hands in silence, the peaked faces of the children. I know there's a mafia at work here. I've seen men on crutches in the dark corners of the underground at the end of the day empty the takings from their fur hats into the bag of their minder.

The next day, as I stand in a queue waiting for a bus to go to Olga's I too receive a touch like the holy woman's kiss.

171

The scene is a picture from hell. The place is black with swarming humanity. A million people live here. Housing blocks mushroom on every spare scrap of ground.

Two small buses arrive, people stampede. One bus however, limps away, its back end scraping the road. Smoke from the exhaust is black in the frosty air. A thick crowd stands forlornly out in the road. People start to flag down cars, holding up the progress of two more buses. It takes so long for people to board one bus that the driver of the coach which has pulled up behind gets impatient. He blasts his horn a couple of times, then gives a nod to the queue behind me and opens the door. The stampede lifts me off my feet. People who have been waiting ahead of me now turn and swarm towards the entrance of the bus as the crowd behind me presses on. I feel as if my arms are about to be broken. I can just about see the driver. He's laughing. The heartlessness of this society gets to me.

I think suddenly of Olga's friend, the murdered singer, Konstantin Ivanov, mercilessly killed in front of his five children. As I'm swept towards the bus, I glance up, beyond the rugby scrum of clawing crowds. There's a sickle moon, silver in the winter dark, and a single star shrouded in cloud. The thought of this man, unknown to me, comes very vividly to me. Strangely, a kind of calm settles in my mind.

The housing blocks rise out of the snow. I remember how appalled I felt when I first saw them, four years ago: the rawness: block after block, no green, nothing. I said then to Olga, 'I'm inviting you to Scotland.' I guess Olga's stuck here now for life...

She tells me she's going to church tomorrow. 'Is it a festival?' I ask, and she explains that she's going to the graveyard where Konstantin Ivanov, the very singer I'd been thinking about at the bus stop, is buried. His requiem has been sung, but tomorrow is to be his *Panikhidra*, the service held forty days after death.

The soul doesn't go to heaven at once, Olga explains, but circles the earth, as the Lord himself did not ascend immediately after his resurrection.

I receive this with a hint of agnosticism. But as I go to bed that night the thought comes to me that perhaps the soul of the murdered singer touched mine in the mad crush that evening as I was being pushed and tugged, lifted off my feet...

I open the New Testament and read in the letter to the Philippians: 'let this mind be in you which was in Christ... who lowered himself [as the Russian text puts it] and became obedient unto death, even the death of the cross...'

As I read I feel the inexplicable, healing brush of an angel's wing, of a mystery I cannot understand.

22

Silver

Anastasia, gentle, ladylike Anastasia, has been knocked off a trolley bus. The rush-hour crowds pushed her backwards just as the driver closed the doors. Her foot caught in the door, the bus drove away, her head cracked against the kerb. She lost consciousness, haemorraged.

I thought; 'This is the end,' she tells me over the phone, repeating several times, 'this is the end'.

'Your guardian angel was looking after you,' I say, and Anastasia agrees, 'God was protecting me.'

Next day her neighbour ordered a taxi, took her to a trauma centre for the treatment of accidents. But they refused to X-ray. 'We have to economize.'

'Perhaps God wanted to punish me,' she says over the phone. 'That's the reason.'

'No,' I say, 'this pitiless society is the reason.'

'Punishing me—and protecting me, then. He knew I needed to get away from the troubles in the school for a while.'

How grieved I feel, that this had to happen to her.

I go out into the snow. My bus disappears before I reach the stop. I wait, another bus pulls up and crowds fight to get out. I see a man's hat fall to the snow. He turns to me, 'Didn't you see it?'

I think he's referring to the bus I've missed. 'No.'

'What kind of society is this? No one sees anything. They hit me, knock my hat off, and you didn't see.'

He's drunk.

'I didn't see,' I repeat.

'You're not from here. Where are you from? One of the republics?'

'No, my country isn't a republic.'

'No hatred,' he said. 'I'm Russian. I invite you. Come home with me. I'll give you tea, a bed... I'm Russian.'

'Thank you.' I peered into the dark, wishing a bus would come.

'I'm Russian. I invite you. I'm Russian.' He was little, his face pinched, obviously the worse for wear. 'They made me cry,' he repeated. His scarf had loosened at his scraggy neck. His glasses misted over. He looked cold. 'I'm Russian,' he kept saying.

'Here's my bus...'

He turned away, and nearly fell flat on the icy road. A pathetic little man, a symbol of this poor, beaten land.

The bus offloads us at its terminus. We cross railway lines. A train is disgorging its passengers, picking up more. People cross the tracks. The driver sounds his horn, moves off into the dark. Old women waddle. I waddle too, for black ice glints in the poor street lights. The place is like a skating-rink.

The pavements away from the metro are less hazardous. There's a thin layer of snow to squeak over. Birches are etched against dim street lights. The streets are paved with silver frost. Silver falls around me, thin snow. Poetically, I think: silver is in the frosty air I breathe. It's nicer to think that, looking at the snowy drizzle, needle-thin in blue-black air, than to think of the pollution I know I also breathe.

There are concerts in the other wing of our building on Sundays. And here we have all the contradictions of this nation with its filth and despair and non-functioning yet loving, giving time to music, poetry, the arts.

The first concert was given by teenagers of about sixteen, pupils at the St Petersburg school for the blind, which draws in blind and partially-sighted children from a wide area, so that many have to board. A bleak future awaits these talented youngsters, sewing mailbags in Dostoyevskian workrooms.

They play rock ballads they've composed themselves. A girl sings, the boys play drums and electric guitar, their faces impassive, their music professional.

Then it's the turn of a thirteen-year-old boy, shy, young for his age. But as soon as he positions himself you know this is an assured performer, and his playing of Chopin is—to my mind—faultless. All done, of course, without looking at any music. And then he plays four pieces he's composed himself.

These moments bring their own silver lining to our lives.

Stuart comes back from Finland with grapefruit, kiwi fruit, bananas, fresh milk, chocolate, toilet rolls—'For a special occasion only!' he warns. I wonder what that might be!

He has had his own experience of something gleaming like silver. Not usually an enthusiast, Stuart waxes lyrical as he talks about the toilet in a health centre in Helsinki. 'Can you imagine what a toilet in heaven would be like? Well, it was there! Shining white. All sorts of helps and devices, rails and things. Gleaming white. Clean!'

Stuart has come back by car. He says the minute they crossed to the Russian side of the border the road was iced over, and an enormous pothole let them know they'd hit home parts once more.

Someone who knows a lot about silver is Philip, who has come here to live and work. He's an artist. His enthusiasm for rebuilding the collapsing house which shelters and feeds us inspires our admiration. So do his candlesticks. They are amazingly beautiful silver pieces.

Philip entertains us to dinner. We eat off pre-revolutionary china (a complete dinner service), and Polish silver—tall dishes with beautiful green fluted glass.

But I feel a shiver as Philip explains it was probably looted. I picture once-lovely houses in Eastern Poland taken over by the Red Army; picture Warsaw, desperate families selling off their treasures to buy bread at exorbitant prices, to buy, perhaps, the chance to escape extermination.

Philip regales us with stories about art dealers with death

threats, bodyguards, rare scoops. People who leave the country with jewellery hidden in their teeth, and elsewhere; who have great treasures in their homes—paintings by Chagal, and other great masters—and fear ever to go out, even with their bodyguards. People who know black marketeers and racketeers who have designed special tops for vodka bottles so that the contents can be poured out and topped up with water or raw spirit, and brand-tops screwed back on. Packets of cigarettes are similarly treated. So is perfume. Sasha and Sonia were duped, buying French perfume and opening it to discover the bottle had been filled with water. Another time Sonia bought a plastic bottle of orange squash, but saw that the top had been tampered with. Brand goods sold at high prices often contain locally produced swillage. And one of the big tragedies is that local stuff is so often swillage.

It seems there are all sorts of ways of finding—and seeking— silver.

23

An Old Northern Town: Vologda

Sonia receives an invitation to go back to her old school: it's forty years since the school was founded. Yelena Sergeyevna, her teacher, is celebrating forty years of teaching—and since Sonia and the others in her class will be forty this year, they have planned to make the anniversary a class reunion.

So, there's good reason to visit her home town and for me to go with her to see an old Russian town. Vladik wants to go too and Sonia agrees.

Vologda, the town Sonia left when she was seventeen to go to St Petersburg to study, is one of the few northern cities whose history goes back to the twelfth century, before the Mongol invasions. It's so deep in the forests that the Germans didn't bomb it. It flourished in the sixteenth century. Ivan the Terrible thought about making it his capital, but a tile slipped from the cathedral roof, and the superstitious Tsar took this as a bad omen and chose Moscow instead. The English came to Vologda as early as 1554, when John Hasse, the agent for the Muscovy Shipping Company, who sent ships each summer to the Northern Dvina River, reported that Vologda was the best place to build warehouses. It was conveniently situated on the banks of the River Vologda, within easy reach of Moscow and Novgorod (yet half the price) and was rich in grain, flax, hemp, wax and lard. Salt, too, was important, along with leather, wool, ironware and wood.

Vologda is still a centre for lacemaking, silver work, wood carving—and I was looking forward to seeing it.

Our train left at 7.30p.m. and was due in at 8.40a.m. Yuri Ivanovich, Sonia's father, would meet us and we'd go straight home, to the good smells of *baboushka's* baking—for Vladik had already let me into the secret: Granny was baking her famous buns.

We awoke to forests—and snow, deeper than any I'd seen in my life, lying thick on the motionless branches of endless pines, thick on the rooftops of wooden houses, thick at the sides of the railway lines.

'There's a little church—I always looked for it when I came home to Vologda...'

Vladik and I lift the half-curtain on the window opposite and peer out, seeing who will be first to spot the landmark.

Yuri Ivanovich insists on carrying my and Sonia's bags. Vladik shoulders a canvas rucksack and we set off down slippery steps, out of the station and across the road for a trolley bus.

The station was built by German prisoners at the end of the war. They built well. The palace-style front of the station rose solid and clean-looking from the snowy pavement. The usual five-storey housing blocks lined the street behind us. The Party Headquarters was beside us. 'I work there,' says Yuri Ivanovich, though he's on a pension. 'They've asked me back.'

'What do you do, Grandad?' Vladik asks.

'Oh, nothing much, just sort papers...'

Old comrades greet Yuri Ivanovich. Already I have caught the feeling of small-town life. Over half a million people live in Vologda, I am told. About the size of Edinburgh, I reckon.

We cross the frozen river which had made Vologda an important centre 500 years before St Petersburg was built. Sonia recalls her mother washing clothes there in the summer. Now, long barges stick out of the ice.

Soon we are passing wooden houses with carved shutters and carved edgings to their roofs, some abandoned, but many well looked after, lived in. Even some of the bus shelters are carved. No beggars, no advertisements, none of the Western lettering which makes the inhabitants of St Petersburg feel like foreigners in their own city (foreigners without a passport).

'Here we are, my wife and I, come back home to end our days in our native town,' says Yuri, seating me at the table in the living-room of their two-room flat.

After the dry summer (and because of mismanagement) the river which saw the rise of Vologda has dried. There's water in homes, schools and hospitals for only a few hours at night. During the day, there's a trickle of cold if you're lucky, otherwise nothing.

Sonia's mother, Valeria Petrovna, got up at two o'clock in the morning to catch the water and bake the cakes which lined the kitchen table.

She is little and round, clearly not well. The temperature in the house is twenty-four degrees. She wears a sleeveless dress. Her face seems waxen, her lips are blue and I hear her breath rasp.

Her cakes are wonderful, made with yeast and stuffed with fried cabbage, or filled with potatoes and sour cream: who could keep slim on such a diet? There are sweet buns too, and cheese, and *tvorog* with sour cream, and slices of fat bacon, all washed down with a special drink, Russian North—a liqueur made from various berries—followed by tea and Vologda sweets, a kind of fudge.

The room is hung with two carpets—Russians carpet their walls rather than their floors, though there is a carpet on the floor too—and wallpaper which Sonia bought and put up for her parents. There are the inevitable bed-settees—two of them—a china cabinet, a dressing-table, all sparkling, thanks to Valeria Petrovna's housewifery.

She left school when she was only fourteen—war-time—to go out to work. She has worked in shops, and life has been a struggle to make ends meet. She sews her own clothes out of hand-me-downs.

'Sonia gave me a blouse,' she says, in her breathless, musical Vologda accent (I noticed a sing-song quality about the endings of the words). 'Do you remember, Sonia? Well, I made these for Papa out of it.' She shows me blue underpants with white dots, neatly laundered, ironed, folded. 'And this will be for your *dacha*, for Vladik's bed.' She shows us a quilt cover, made from a sheet gone thin in the middle.

Sonia has brought shoes which need to be heeled. Yuri Ivanovich can heel shoes, but we need to buy little metal tips.

The table gets put back. Papa goes back to work, Vladik watches the old black-and-white television set. We transfer to the kitchen to sit on the usual small, square stools which supply the seating needs of every single kitchen I've been in. We drink coffee and talk. About school, about the forthcoming evening, about the chicken Valeria Petrovna wants her daughter to prepare, about the lack of water. They have filled the bath and buckets and jars.

Sonia tells me that in her last three school years the girls in the class ran a boycott against her. No one spoke to her.

'Why?'

'Jealousy. One of them, Zoya, needed my help last summer to coach her son. So she phoned me out of the blue, and of course I helped her. But she's never been to see me, never got in touch, even though her son passed the exams and got into university in St Petersburg.'

'What about your teacher? You liked her so much.'

'I never mentioned it. But last time I went to see her Zoya was there too, and she said, "Why did we all hate Sonia Yurevna?"'

'She said that? Right in front of you?'

'That's right. "Why did we all hate Sonia Yurevna?" And Yelena Sergeyevna said: "You were jealous".'

Sonia's blue eyes filled with tears. 'Once, our class had to go and work on a collective farm. For a whole month. They all ganged up against me, the boys too. I ran away. I walked and walked, through our Vologda countryside. It began to get dark. And there was nothing: no houses, no proper roads. Nothing. So in the end I turned back. The teacher gave me a row for causing them trouble... Sasha says I mustn't try to seek my revenge. I should be modest, simple, quiet. So I haven't brought anything special to wear. I've brought you. You're my defence.'

We walk into town. Sonia walks with a swinging grace, the result of a childhood on skis. The air is crisp and pure. The sun is shining. People are on skis, on sledges.

Sunlight gleams on the golden domes of the cathedral. Churches line the skyline.

Lenin's sister was exiled to Vologda—her brother's statue scowls from the edge of gardens as we leave the shops where we've managed to get Vladik a pair of trousers, thick and coarse: the ones he has are in holes at the knee.

We head for historic Vologda. The Vologda kremlin has disappeared but the ancient panorama of golden domes remains, including those of the sixteenth-century cathedral, soon to be reopened.

'There were a hundred and seventy churches in Vologda,' a museum guide explains.

And indeed English visitors in the seventeenth century noticed the custom of building two parish churches, one, unheated, for summer, the other for use in winter. Nearly all were of wood, as were the houses—pine logs with birch cladding—and on the roofs, as a protection against the ever-present hazard of fire, turf.

We find the museum guide in a room in the former Archbishop's residence. She explains that the museum itself is shut, but she will be only too happy to show us round in a day or two.

We walk back out into the gathering dusk.

'Don't you see what an asset you'll be to our school celebrations?' Sonia says to me. 'Just think—in Vologda—someone from the West.'

Sonia is planning to make a splash. She'll make a speech and produce me, her pupil. Now we need to buy a present for the teacher, if not for the school. We head for a bookshop. Before perestroika you couldn't buy Western authors, apart from the chosen few. Now you can buy only foreign books; good Russian literature seems to have disappeared. A sign of the times.

We see a book about the Bible, but it turns out to be a

translation from a Hungarian author addressed 'to my Soviet readers'.

It's mainly concerned to debunk miracles.

On the door of the Post Office is a notice that there is a Bible Marathon: everyone in Vologda will receive a copy of *The Book of Life*—the four Gospels in modern Russian, run together to make a single book. Anyone who wants to study the Bible more seriously is invited to a meeting in the evening.

Inside the Post Office a man's face beaming from another poster offers eternal joy.

And the citizens of Vologda, including Yuri Ivanovich and Valeria Petrovna, read horoscopes (half the back page of the local paper, *Red North* is full of Nostrodamus' predictions for the last years of the twentieth century). They also follow the teachings of a bearded man who believes you can heal everything by going into the forest and breathing in the fresh air, taking deep breaths, thinking of the pure sources from which all this bounty comes. And plunging into cold water twice a day—the colder the healthier.

'They're quite right,' Valeria Petrovna says, breathlessly. 'Did you see the programme on television where they were breaking the ice and putting babies into the water? I should do that too: out in the snow and a cold-water douche.'

'That's my mother for you,' Sonia says, later. 'She won't go outside all winter, for fear of catching a cold and getting another bad asthma attack, but she thinks you can go and roll in the snow without any harm.'

Yelena Sergeyevna, Sonia's teacher, has suffered a terrible loss. Her son, an electric train driver, was killed in a head-on collision with another train when he was twenty-six. He'd married a woman with a young child, they had a child of their own—and he was wiped out. Yelena Sergeyevna's whole life changed. Her room became a shrine to her dead son. His photographs cover the walls and, says Sonia, she goes to the graveyard every day. Every single day ...

Last time Sonia said goodbye to her, she looked back to wave and saw that Yelena Sergeyevna was making the sign of the cross over her.

'There's a chapel in the graveyard. Services are held there all the time. I'm sure she goes there to pray.'

'Why do you think she let you suffer...? She must have known.'

'Yes. That time with Zoya she said, "I should have done something to help you".'

'And you never ever said anything to her, even though you were so close.'

'Never. I couldn't.'

The second of February dawned... In Poland it's the Feast of Candlemas, the day when people take down their Christmas decorations. In Soviet Russia it is the Day of the School. Sonia and I head for the Russian *banya*, the bathhouse, walking through the snow among wooden houses. Birch trees point slender branches to the crisp blue sky. Birds sing. The sun shines. This, I tell Sonia, is how I've always imagined a Russian town. I thoroughly agree with the people who advised Peter the Great not to build a city in the low-lying swamps on the banks of the Neva. But he needed his access to the sea, and so we have muck and mosquitoes and a damp, damp climate. And all the misery and poverty of Dostoyevsky's Petersburg.

There's none of that here. You can breathe freely, take life slowly, feel the presence of this thing, nature, that Russians love so much.

'The Vologda bathhouse is small, just like in a village,' Sonia explains. 'No sauna, no pool of cold water, only one shower. But you get a good steam.'

It is just after 9a.m. A woman is sitting cooling off in the changing rooms, a towel around her shoulders. I think that there's not much about me to indicate I am a Westerner, and once my clothes are off there will be no difference at all. Except, perhaps, the amount of flesh.

Inside, the bathhouse is simplicity itself. We look out onto trees and pavements. Newspaper between the lower double frames keep us hidden from the street. There is indeed only one shower. Everyone has brought their own basins. Women are soaping themselves and rinsing off, pouring water over themselves. Sonia fills a basin with water to soak our birch leaves for the beating session to follow in the dark wooden steam room where hot air fills my nostrils. We spread out pieces of rag on the seat and sit down to sweat out dirt, disease, bad thoughts.

One woman is already sitting on the bench. Two others follow us in and stand, switching themselves.

The woman beside us asks Sonia to beat her with birch leaves. 'Thank you,' she says. 'May God give you health.'

That's what I hear over and over again as the Vologda women rub each other's backs: '*Daj vam Bog zdorovije...*'

On the way home I ask Sonia: 'Did they say that when you were small and came here?' 'Yes,' she says. '*Daj vam Bog zdorovije...* They all said it, even then.'

I reflect how Leninism and Stalinism, which closed the churches and silenced the prayers, couldn't kill the essential heart of 'holy Russia'—which, like the Celtic tradition, is for the whole person, the person unclothed...

It takes longer for sweat to show on me: Sonia suggests it's to do with the amount of fat one carries around—though she's far from large; also because I go so seldom to the *banya*, whereas she went in St Petersburg only last week. They had no hot water in their flat...

Then outside to soap and take turns under the shower.

I can well imagine how Valeria Petrovna spends three hours here once a week. She has her spot where she always sits, resting between soaping and steaming. And I can understand how the bathhouse is a place of relaxation for women especially. Here one has only oneself to think of. Here too, neighbours help each other. Solid women who would push you out of the way in overcrowded public transport, naked, offer goodwill to one another.

We use our birch twigs—and as we switch and rub the smell of the forest comes to our nostrils. No packaged essence: just the good pungent smell of birches.

Outside in the changing room I offer my Western lotions. Guerlain's fragrances in the Vologda bathhouse! Women comment: 'Where's the nice smell from?'

'We've got a celebration today,' Sonia explains.

'In a restaurant?' they wonder.

An elderly woman pulls a white belt around a thin, shapeless dress which serves as a petticoat. Is this for a hernia, perhaps? But no, it is her corsets. She fastens suspenders, pulls up woollen stockings.

We trudge home through sun and snow.

'With light steam,' Granny gives us the traditional greeting as she opens the door.

We drink tea, have cabbage soup, look at photographs: the wedding photographs in the Palace of Weddings, the registering of the births, photographs of Papa in his Red Army uniform at the end of the war: I note his tunic-style shirt. One of Sonia's grandfather shows the old man wearing the same style shirt we associate with traditional Russia. I say, it's a pity men don't wear these shirts still.

'It's seventy years...' she says. 'So much was destroyed.'

I stretch out on the bed-settee. Sonia paints her nails. 'Do you know how long I've had this varnish?' she asks. 'Eighteen years— since my student days.'

I plug in my heated curling-brush, to the delight of Vladik, who remembered this new technology from our holiday in the south.

But we still have no presents, and no speech. An old school friend, Ilya, will bring flowers from the rest of the class.

'What does Ilya do?' I wonder.

Sonia looks at me strangely. 'He works for the KGB.'

I try not to show my reaction. 'How do you know?' I ask.

'He told us himself... Does that make you feel scared?'

'No,' I lie. 'Not really. Why does he do it?'

'Well, he's capable, ambitious, in a small town like Vologda...' I understood. 'Anyway,' Sonia continues. 'I'm sure every country needs its secret service. For its own defence.'

'Yes, but...' I say no more.

There is a six-storey building in St Petersburg which is now pointed out to tourists—the headquarters of the KGB. 'We say: there are six storeys above ground which we can see—and twelve storeys below which no one sees,' the guide explains. But a friend sitting beside me on one particular tour said, 'I knew the son of the architect of that building. He was killed as soon as he'd completed the plans.' 'Killed?' 'He knew too much...'

'I've asked Ilya to get our return tickets for us,' Sonia goes on. 'So he'll come back here afterwards.'

As she boils wax rollers to put into her luxuriant auburn hair Sonia explains the way she imagines the evening will be: a ceremonious gathering, with the teachers lined up on the platform, to which former pupils will be invited to say a few words about themselves and what they have done since leaving school.

Which is when she intends to produce me.

However, when we get to the school, it turns out to be very different. Except for the attitude of Sonia's classmates.

I recognize them at once, without any introduction, a bunch of women dressed up to the nines, standing, as it happens, between the main door and the cloakroom. One of them smiles at Sonia, greets her. The others stare in stony silence.

I suppose I'm getting used to Russian extremism. Westerners would hide their hatred with cool smiles—and plenty of chat afterwards: 'She hasn't changed her hairstyle since she was at school. And what a frumpy suit she was wearing. My dear, I'm sure she bought that blouse in a department for ten-year-olds. And what about that foreign woman she had with her...' Sonia does not introduce me and I realize she is waiting for her moment of glory when all will be revealed.

It doesn't come.

Instead, we are treated to a school concert, which unfortunately we can't see, because the old raised stage has gone, and can't hear, because the large crowd are all prepared for a reunion of former classmates and teachers and chatters noisily, catching up with news.

Another former pupil called Sasha sits at the end of the row. 'You're nervous,' he says to Sonia, 'are you going to perform?'

'I'm going to say a poem for Yelena Sergeyevna.'

'How could you, in front of this crowd? It's better to keep your private thoughts for friends.'

'But,' says, Sonia afterwards, 'for me it's quite the reverse: I could have said that poem in public, but in the small group afterwards I held back and couldn't say a thing about myself.'

That, of course, is what makes her a good teacher: the ability to project herself in front of an audience.

I sit in between Sonia and Ilya, who is armed with flowers for his teacher. He greets me with something about: 'The inhabitants of St Petersburg in Vologda.' I'm not sure what to say, and Sonia leans forward, sparkling mischievously. 'I didn't tell you, Ilya, about my secret. Jenny is from Scotland.'

'Oh!' he says. And in English, 'How do you do?'

Thereafter he calls me Jennifer. In Russia, diminutives are only for close friends who use the 'thou' form—*ty*, while the more polite form is full name and patronymic with the 'you' form—*vy*. I notice all these former classmates, although they haven't seen each other for years, still use the informal 'thou' and diminutive. Ilya and I are strangers. But I wonder how he knows the full form of my name, which to Russian ears sounds as if it should be Yevgenia.

He is relaxed, a little too friendly, kissing the ladies' hands. Elena Sergeyevna leaves her seat among the teachers in the front rows and comes to greet her former pupils.

She wears a black blouse, her greying hair drawn tightly back into a firm plaited bun, her blue eyes sparkling. She greets me warmly and at the end of the concert when no reunions have taken place she says, 'Go up to my class, and we'll talk there. Bring her,' she says, smiling at me, 'she's one of ours too'. There are vigorous gypsy dances. The girls wear traditional floral scarfs and swirling skirts. Then they do a stately folk dance. The costumes here are rich and brilliant, gold and red embroidery, high hats, shawls, long skirts. Younger children tell folk tales and sing. They wear peasant costume from the region: the girls in red blouses, red beads, blue dresses; the boys in embroidered belted tunics with full sleeves.

A choir of little boys (Russian children start school at six or seven and continue for ten years, so little ones are taught in the same building as teenagers) gets up to sing. 'This song will show you the new atmosphere in our school,' their teacher says.

They sing about the love and mercy of the Lord.

Afterwards I listen while the others, up in their teacher's room, swap reminiscences about their schooldays. Sonia is very quiet. It occurs to me that Yelena Sergeyevna might well have realized the reason why Sonia has brought me to this evening and have given her the chance to introduce her Western guest. But she doesn't, and we keep quiet, exchanging smiles at the way our plans have come to naught.

'It's just as well,' we agree afterwards.

'We say in Russian: Man proposes, God disposes,' Sonia says as we walk arm in arm to the trolley stop. 'Better to be modest.'

I can see she's upset. Not at the failure of her plans, but that the old enmity still continues after all these years.

'And,' Ilya and she agree as we walk over frozen snow towards her parents' flat, 'it's a pity no one had a chance to talk to the teachers. That's what we wanted, not a school concert... Look at this...' Sonia breaks off. 'It's just what Mama believes in.'

A little girl no older than eight or nine, dressed only in her pants, runs out into the snow, pours a basin of water over herself and runs back inside...

We go upstairs. Valeria Petrovna and Yuri Ivanovich are waiting. Vladik is ready for bed. 'Well, how was it? Come in, tea's ready.'

We sit round the kitchen table, holding a post-mortem on the evening.

'Times have changed,' says Yuri Ivanovich. 'No one makes speeches or praises one another any more. Mediocrity. That's all.'

Sonia goes to see to Vladik in the other room. Ilya asks, 'Did Sonia tell you what service I'm engaged in?'

'Yes.'

'You don't feel scared?'

'No.' Again, this isn't true. I don't feel comfortable, that's for sure. 'I'd like to know—though of course I quite understand if you can't tell me—what exactly you do.'

He says something about 'securing commercial and business enterprises'.

Ilya's son studies at a boys' school deep in the forest. They concentrate on the outdoor life. Birds of prey feed from their hands. They also specialize in business studies, computers, languages. It so happens, his wife teaches there too.

I think: yes, and who gets to study at a school like that? What service are the boys being prepared for? There are no answers to questions it's not wise to ask.

Ilya says he's been to London once. 'Just for a couple of days—on holiday.' And Paris, twice.

'Of course,' says Yuri Ivanovich afterwards, 'we get these holiday trips to the West as well.'

Ilya has to start work next morning at eight o'clock. He excuses himself early.

'Sonia,' I say, 'I want to talk to you. About Ilya.'

'What do you want to know?'

'When he went to London—it wasn't a holiday, was it?'

'No,' she says, 'but it wasn't anything against England. It was in a group.'

'To spy on someone?'

'To spy on someone,' she agrees.

Perhaps as an atonement we go to church next morning. The service is ending. A woman scolds us: 'What do you mean, coming when the prayers are over?'

The church has just been returned, stripped of its icons—the ancient frescoes were scraped from the walls. Yet, once again, as in the rush hour crowds outside Pioneer Metro Station, I feel the brush of the angel wing and I'm filled with wonder that now, at this moment, in this poor, disfigured church I am... And the host of heaven is... And God the Lord... The little church has been through its own Calvary. Maybe that's why, now, I feel this touch of something that belongs to eternity...

True to her word, the guide shows us the museum: rich displays of lace, tablecloths, waistcoats, peasants' dress; lace for church use—altar cloths, coverings for Communion vessels. And sixteenth-century icons which glow with colour. Sonia comments that they are full of joy.

The most amazing of all, awesome in its simplicity, is an early fourteenth-century Mother of God with her Child—faded yellow paint, the Child's cheek curved up against the Mother's. His fingers curl about the edging of her veil. But he doesn't look at the Mother. His head is thrust back. His grave eyes look outward. At the world. At me. And the Mother is full of serenity, a deep peace. Her eyes look inward, reflect untold suffering, compel. Like pools of water reflecting an endless sky. The icon radiates an awesome tenderness, purity. I do not want to go away.

The guide opens the museum shop specially for us to buy souvenirs. Some Americans come and they are let in too.

And then it's goodbye to Vologda, to Sonia's parents. Valeria Petrovna says, 'I'm glad about your friendship.' I leave her my New Testament.

Yuri Ivanovich goes with us to the station. Our bags are heavier than before: Sonia has brought her mother coffee; she goes back with potatoes they have grown themselves, a cabbage, cream, boiled eggs and cutlets for our food on the train.

The train is already standing on the tracks—but it's too much to hope the ladies in charge of each compartment will let us in much before the departure time. We prepare for a long wait in the snow. However, after only five minutes the door opens, steps are let down and we go inside. Our coach is carpeted and clean. And now we realize that this is the special coach for special people.

'You and I,' Yuri Ivanovich always speaks to me as though he's talking to a child, 'go to buy tickets. They say—"There aren't any." We have to argue and cajole and perhaps we get a seat. But the head of Ilya's department always has a few spare tickets at his disposal. Ilya just has to phone the ticket office and he gets the tickets.'

In this supposedly equal society, some are markedly more equal than others.

Sonia and I read Mark's Gospel, while Vladik draws Disney cartoon characters with felt-tip pens and our companion, who builds electric power stations, dozes in the top bunk. And so we travel back to St Petersburg...

24

Lenten Days

For days now Stuart has had severe pain down one side of his head. He develops unsightly sores which I paint with Russian green. This green is perhaps something like gentian violet. You see people with daubings on cold sores, on cuts. Sasha hunts through the stores in the Military Hospital for antibiotics, finds enough to start Stuart off but not enough to complete the course.

I go into town and buy exotic tea packaged in Finland for dollars. The girl, whose cold is as bad as mine, lets me smell the various brands of tea. The scent of lemon decides me. I see Gouda cheese at $9 and go across to a milk products shop for Russian cheese in roubles. It now costs £2 a kilo—and is tasteless. The girl says they haven't managed to let it ripen. I go away cheeseless, and because I haven't remembered to bring a jam jar I can't buy sour cream either. A customer with a dripping nose is selling jam jars. I wait hopefully, but the assistant complains, 'They're dirty,' and I see they are, so I draw a blank here too. However, I buy oranges and two grapefruit for our health.

Metro fares have gone up over 100 per cent without warning. Nina comes round and tells me that with any other nation such price rises would have brought the govenment down. Here, silence. The changes are staggering, and the worst hit are pensioners who only stand to lose...

Things are awful in the school—the children play table tennis at every break, wear themselves out, don't concentrate on lessons, don't do homework. In a word, they don't care! All the complaints which were hurled at us by the breakaway group seem sadly true: there's no discipline because there's no leadership. Meantime, however, the Bible classes continue twice a week, necessitating hours of preparation for me. Phone calls come from abroad using us as a resource. I stagger off to wash dishes in dirty water. My nose feels the size of a football, my face is covered in blotchy spots. Stop, world, I want to get off...

It's the eve of Orthodox Lent, and we happened to be in church when a wedding was being held, we guessed, before the fast. It used to be that all pleasures, public and private, were forbidden during Lent and a child conceived during the fast would be given a non-Christian name. However, the old Russian language was kind to children born out of wedlock. Such a child would be named Bogdan, God-given. The surname still exists today.

During the seventy-year fast of official atheism, few if any church weddings were held. Then, in the seventies, young couples, the children of highly-placed Communists, the cream of young Soviet intelligentsia, newly come to faith, chose to honour their marriage with the blessing of the church, to kiss the crown the priest put on their heads, to kiss the ring which bound them in wedlock, the icons, each other, while old women looked on amazed, wondering aloud whether the two young people were foreigners.

Nowadays everyone wants to get married in church, though in this case the guests who stood around obviously couldn't understand what was going on. However, the bride and groom were involved in a dance of elaborate gesture and movement: they held right hands and the priest spread his stole over them and led them down the aisle and then three times around the church, up to the opened Royal Doors (which look into the sanctuary as if into the heart of heaven), kissing the icons on the right and on the left. The prayers were chanted in Old Church Slavonic; the Bible reading, which was sung, was hard to follow. The priest dropped the wedding ring. I hoped no one would regard it as a bad omen...

Crowds of grannies pushed about, doing their own thing, organizing lists of petitionary prayers, talking loudly, while the couple walked forward (and the carpet on which they stood was rolled up behind them so that no one else would make it dirty) and the priest gave them each a crown, making the sign of the cross over them with each crown in his right hand, offering it to them to kiss, then putting a crown on each heads, so that they wore crowns throughout the marriage ceremony.

The priest was young and plump, with an air of boredom. He wore the usual velvet hat, which he removed to sing the Gospel reading—and to our amazement and amusement publicly combed his hair ... It was his day, not the bride's, and indeed, hardly had the ceremony finished when the next couple was lining up for their turn on the carpet—just like in the old Palaces of Weddings under the Soviets.

Does anything change? Stuart thinks: no. Gloomily he says, 'The West pours in its millions. It all gets sucked into the Russian swamp—and nothing changes.'

However, Philip (our friend who dines off silver) treated us to a meal out in a restaurant last Thursday. Other guests were present, all Russians, the women dressed most elegantly in chic, swinging mini-skirts. Flowers were delivered to their table. So some people have money—and indeed, those with access to dollars obviously live well.

I decided it's been too long since we ate any salad, so I went off to the market near the Vladimirskaya Church. I bought tomatoes, cucumber, lettuce... I was buying bananas when a woman came up. 'Don't buy them here,' she said. 'They're a third of the price round the corner.' She took me off round the corner and right enough, there were bananas in a shop and a cucumber too, so I bought them there. She said, 'How do you cope with all the difficulties of our life?' I said, 'The hardest thing is being away from my family.'

But it's hard to see the distress and poverty. Like just now. While I was in the market buying the tomatoes, an old woman hovered round the stall. 'Hey, granny, move on, there's nothing for you here,' the stallholder said. I knew the tomatoes cost half her month's pension and I followed her, wanting to give her some. But in the end I didn't dare, just gave some rouble notes to two other grannies begging.

A friend from Moscow said an old lady came up to her and said, 'Please give me something, I'm hungry.'

A young woman, maybe twenty-two, hair blonde-streaked, sits on the ground in the metro underpass, holds a child, holds out her hand. People stop to take a second look. Is she sick? Desperate? Or part of a mafia with the child used as a tear-jerker?

The other day in swirling snow I saw an old blind woman begging in the street, a child tied to her with a rope.

However, if I feel dismayed at the contradictions of St Petersburg—the glory of its palaces, the misery of life on the streets; the severity of long dark winters and the amazing light of lengthening evenings, until in the end darkness seems to disappear altogether—I'm in good company. The nineteenth-century writer Alexander Herzen wrote in the 1840s in an article, *Moscow and Petersburg*: 'Nowhere have I been given to so many sad thoughts so often as in Petersburg. Suffocated with heavy doubts I wandered around its granite and was near to despair. Those moments have bound me to St Petersburg and because of them I have fallen in love with it.'

Winter drags on, and on. It's light earlier—and stays light till almost seven. But snow and ice continue. There are no buds on the trees, no small flowers poking up in little gardens—no little gardens for them to poke up into—no green. I carry a bowl of dirty dishes along our corridor to wash them as usual in the bathroom—we spread a board over the bath and put the washing-up bowl on top. Sometimes I try to pretend I'm walking along the corridor of a stately home.

Today Shakespeare comes to my mind as I wash dishes in the bathroom. 'And thou away, the very birds seem mute, Or if they sing, 'tis with so dull a cheer/That leaves look pale, dreading the winter's near.' The music lifts my heart. 'Dull a cheer'... The audacity of that choice of those two particular words makes a melody which sings across the centuries. I think of Anna Grigorevna, the English teacher here, who hasn't been giving the kids grammar because there aren't any textbooks, so they've been learning Blake by heart.

Besides, Cupid is at work in the eighth class; sweet thirteen loves even the non-existent spring.

25

The World at Our Door

Yesterday our afternoon went like this. There was a knock at the door. Alex, the teacher who is involved with blind children, came in with two women and a man. Suddenly our room seemed very full. There were no introductions but I understood the younger woman was an interpreter, the others were American.

'I've brought them to see you,' Alex said, 'because Arlene's grandmother was Scottish, and I wondered if Stuart might know her.'

'Welsh, actually,' Arlene explained.

But Welsh or Scottish was all the same to Alex, who sat smiling happily while Stuart, working in our inner room, kept himself well hidden away.

'I just love Russia,' Arlene enthused. 'All those treasures. But the greatest treasure is the people. I just feel so much love for them.'

I wondered if my silence was a bit deafening, but luckily Arlene had plenty to say. 'I'm living now. I've never really lived before. Even the conditions, standing in line ... they just teach me what's really important in life.'

Alex doesn't speak English, and she doesn't speak Russian, so I wasn't sure how they'd got to know each other; but here they were, so I made tea and put out something for them to eat. Her husband gave up his building business to come here, she said.

'I didn't know what it would be like,' he said. 'Politics colour your attitude. But I thought that behind all the propaganda were people and I just had to come.'

Arlene agreed: 'When you know the truth it changes everything...'

They used the words 'the truth' a lot. 'We're here to help Russians find the truth,' they said.

The problem was, we were going out to the theatre in the evening, to very special seats. So as soon as the visitors disappeared, I stripped off and put on a dressing-gown, trying to get along for a shower before we went out to the theatre. But Sonia appeared, hassled after a long session with Lena. I tried to cheer her up, 'Never mind, do you know the greatest treasure there is— Russian people.' She laughed. 'Even with all our contradictions!'

We sat down to renewed cups. But then came another knock at the door. Three more people stood in the corridor. One was a priest in cassock and cross—it turned out he was Dutch, with two Dutch friends. Sonia whispered, 'And you're not even dressed.' But I was beyond caring. The whole world comes, constantly, smiling: 'Here I am in Russia! Help me, let me use your phone, translate for me, do you know where I can find...?' Russians come to find the foreigners. 'Is Bob here? Can he take a letter? A parcel? He wanted me to help him buy a fur hat, an icon...' No one passes us by. So let them take us as we are, dressed or not.

We made some more coffee, opened some more biscuits, talked. 'Why did you become Orthodox?' we asked Father Feodor, and he replied simply, 'It's the best way there is.'

The guests we'd just waved off think their way is the best way too... However, Father Feodor wasn't trying to prove a point, he was just replying to a question. He trained in the Spiritual Academy here in the seventies, when it was a hotbed of KGB men. I asked about KGB attitudes to him and he laughed, 'They couldn't understand why I, a chemist, should want to become a priest.'

He'd been brought up in the Dutch West Indies, he said, went to Holland to study and found that Vatican II had changed the Catholic Church in Holland beyond all recognition. Friends recommended the Orthodox Church. 'There's mysticism there,' they'd said. 'And incense.' So he went along and decided to become Orthodox. He went back home to see his parents. 'Go to church and pray and you'll know the right thing to do,' they said.

Out of the blue, family friends asked if he'd like to join them on their yacht, sailing back to Holland. On the way, out in the ocean, he felt that he should become a priest.

'I spoke to an Orthodox priest about it. I said, I'm not even baptized Orthodox and yet I have this calling to be a priest.'

The priest had smiled. 'If you can cross an ocean in a little boat I'm sure there's nothing to stop you from becoming a priest,' he'd said.

So he wrote to the seminary in St Petersburg and fifteen months later received a letter granting acceptance. He spent three years studying here to become a priest.

And that was all very interesting—but we still had to get ready for the theatre and we must not be late because we had been given the best seats in the Tsar's own box for a performance of a new ballet...

The composer too has come to our building. His name is Alexander. His father was a Count from Transylvania—but Alexander imbibes not blood but varieties of Chinese tea that he brews for us in a clay pot he carries with him specially. He's a lute player and serenades us with Byrd and Dowland. He lives in a room along the corridor without any carpets on the floor, a single crucifix on the wall. And he has come to our door, with the generous invitation to a performance of his latest ballet, *Macbeth*. Going to the Russian theatre is magnificent enough—but to be honoured with the best seats in the Tsar's box...

We went to the Maly Teatr with its glittering chandeliers and sumptuous decor, and sat comfortably in the central box, leaning our elbows on soft golden velour.

The ballet was danced to an interesting blend of classical and medieval instruments, including recorders. The score included echoes of Elizabethan and earlier music, reflecting Alexander's own researches.

During the interval I derived much fascination from looking at the women and little girls: floating black lace, velvet, chiffon, gold and silver lamé. Nowadays some young women wear the briefest of black mini-dresses. Long hair tumbles loose or is gathered up into a variety of elaborate clasps and combs. Little girls wear elaborate white bows in their hair.

We noticed the number of young couples and young families generally in the theatre. Does this reflect a cultured nation, or simply a lack of choice of other entertainment?

Whatever the answer—Alexander has given us an evening we shall never forget.

26

Laying Up Treasure

We haven't eaten cheese for a long time (strictly, it's forbidden in Orthodox Lent). When I came out of the metro today I glanced in the windows of the kiosk closest to the station and I saw some cheese. Camembert, for less than £1. I hesitated, then hurried on. Coming home later in the evening I noticed the cheese still there, tempting me. The kiosk was in darkness, but a young woman was still sitting there, her little sliding window half open, a soldier in uniform beside her. The need in me to buy things is, I've noticed, greater than the need to consume. It's a bit like the way I sprayed on perfume in the dirty school. A sort of escapism. But quite hazardous. For a start, you need to be an economist to cope with all the different currencies. An expert linguist, too. I still find Russian numbers difficult to understand.

Even Russians sometimes make mistakes. We bought some bananas today. The young man in the street insisted on showing off his English—and said 815 roubles instead of 850. He wanted to correct this, but we held him to the price and he good-naturedly gave way, losing out on the deal.

Now I wondered if I would be the loser. Remembering Philip's stories of brand-goods being opened and inferior stuff put in, I asked if I could look at the cheese I was buying—and found a sealed tin inside the cardboard box. People were already crowding round the booth as I warily pulled a thousand-rouble note out of my wallet. 'Be careful, they'll cheat you,' warned another young man. 'Count the change. Are you a foreigner?' he went on. 'Where are you from?' He was becoming too friendly. His shoulders rubbed mine as I left the booth. 'Have you any old rags for sale? Jeans, you know... Don't be afraid,' he added as I edged away. 'I tried to make sure they weren't cheating you.'

'They stole all our things,' I told him.

'Stole them? Russians stole them?'

This was the last stage of the saga of the stranded Leith ship... It came, but to Riga, Latvia, and with a new crew. How were we to get our stuff? (We only have visas to leave the country, not to get back in.) A truck was arranged, a friend, a driver. There were borders to be crossed, with visas at $10 per person a throw, petrol to be bought (stolen, it was claimed, by Estonian guards). The men said they slept four days in a lorry in freezing conditions while they waited for permission to cross, only to find our stuff dispelled around Riga: a typewriter in the office of the shipowner himself. They said they got a fur coat off a woman's back and rescued everything, except for one tea chest—and one boot.

Stuart paid out hundreds of roubles and dollars. The man eventually brought our boxes and trunks. I optimistically cleared spaces in our overcrowded rooms while Stuart helped carry the boxes upstairs, finding the load very much lighter than the one he'd manhandled across the docks in Edinburgh. Locks were broken off trunks, tea chests re-sealed with a different sort of tape from the kind we'd used. Even so, we still hoped, poor trusting fools, that we'd find some of our things.

There was nothing. The boxes were crammed full of the sort of old stuff you buy in the flea markets. Food, toiletries, casseroles, fur coats, clothes, books, even cassocks and a wooden cross— everything had gone. A thousand pounds' worth of stuff, we reckoned. Only, by some miracle, Stuart's Russian typewriter survived, plus a hand-weave skirt, a bit out of shape, an artificial-fur coat and a single stray tin of instant marmalade. Not a lot for all that money.

So we weren't very happy, sorrowing at this abuse of the kindness of people who had donated so much to help people here, and feeling to the full the meaning of the idiom 'to add insult to injury' as we thought of more than £300 paid out to get this rubbish transported from Riga.

Who was the thief? Who knows? The waters around that particular cargo seem very murky. All sorts of hints and accusations are being made by crew members against one another. We've got to the stage where we really don't want to know.

'Lay not up treasures on earth where... thieves break in and steal,' I teach the children.

Nothing has changed since the days when a crowd in Galilee first heard those wise and gentle words. Only here, where crime was once suppressed, unseen, does it now shock everyone by its blatant openness.

No, nothing has changed. But the text continues: 'Lay up for yourselves treasure in heaven.' And a colleague called by to tell us this was happening too. This evening there was to be a service in which monks would be professed.

A hundred years ago, as I see from old prints, engravings and paintings of St Petersburg, it was by no means unusual to see nuns swathed in black walking the streets in the company of high-born ladies, priests in their cassocks, and monks in black head-dresses.

Now it almost never happens, so off we went, slithering across the paths in the park where we used to run with the children last autumn, and into the chapel in the Spiritual Academy.

The whole place was in darkness: only the flames of thin yellow candles gave the dim light by which black-robed monks in high hats and veils formed a procession, virtually carrying in two novices. The novices, we later learnt, were aged only twenty-one and twenty-three. Their parents were nowhere in evidence, though a little boy of about nine—who may have been a relative—was running around the side. No women sang in the choir, so the balcony upstairs where the women's choir normally stands was empty. We went up there for a better view, and stood looking down on the congregation, standing crowded together in the darkness, lit only by the gleam of candleshine.

The service was very sombre, funereal—the monk is leaving the world, being buried, to re-emerge with a new name, a new way of life. I was disturbed, not so much that the boys can hardly know the world they are leaving, as by the fact that, although a monk is, of course, supposed to be totally humble (the sermon, based on Christ's command, 'take my yoke upon you', stressed that obedience is even more important than prayer), there's a sense in which by keeping him so very far apart he is made out to be someone special. So much so that laypeople—and particularly women—are forever felt to be on a lower level.

What is open to the monk, however, is high service in the church (the top jobs are reserved for the celibate) and maybe, too, the hidden life of holiness which has smouldered at the heart of Orthodoxy for a thousand years.

The boys were called Arkady and Nikolai. They were escorted in, quite literally 'under wraps', muffled from head to toe in black veils, so that I couldn't see them at all at first, only hear their voices making their vows. Then they were unwrapped, and their white cassocks marked them out in the dimly-lit church.

They were given one item after another of monastic clothing: black robes, a rope for their waist, possibly a prayer rope—I couldn't see it all, high on the balcony, looking dizzyingly down at the black-robed men below.

Each time the boys kissed the clothing they were given and kissed the hand of the priest giving it. I heard the sound of metal—and guessed this was scissors for the cutting of the hair. (The monk is offered scissors three times, and three times he humbly hands them over to another monk, showing his acceptance of the shaving to come.) However, it turned out that this cutting of hair was symbolic. It was followed by the donning of the high hat, and now the boys were monks; they stood fully robed, each holding a candle and a wooden cross.

We found the sermon hard to follow—the priest's diction was poor because of lack of education. This was a deliberate policy a couple of generations ago: educated men were not supposed to enter the church.

Standing in his veils and high hat, the clergyman who led the service, one of the older members of staff in the Spiritual Academy, looked for all the world like pictures I've seen of the ancient Jewish High Priest. He brought the new monks forward, kissed them both three times (Russians always kiss with the right cheek first, something I've had to learn). Then he left the church and the two new monks stood in front of the congregation and received the kisses of the other monks, priests and choir—no women.

The picture now was a formal bowing and bending of those high black hats (one boy kept straightening his) in the threefold kiss. There were still no lights, and there was no music, though unaccompanied male voices had sung ancient chants all through the service—like voices from another world; the church's gift to these boys who were giving everything.

The monastic vows are threefold: humility, patience or long-suffering, and obedience. The understanding of this tradition is that Christians aren't meant to be active, but to receive everything as the will of God. So there has been no precedent for active Christian involvement in areas of peace, justice or human need. The church in Russia has not been active in social change.

This is why Lena's energy and Boris's vision in getting our school started, getting and maintaining the building, is something not to be despised. In its own way, whatever the faults of organization, this school is actively laying up treasure in heaven by creating something good here on earth. It is seen in this way by the parents who send their children here. It is certainly seen in this light by the children, who all agree how much they like their school.

27

A Quiet Unspoilt Place

There are no state holidays for Easter, the most important of all Russian festivals, but schools have almost two weeks off at the end of March. Our school will just have a week because we observe Easter.

The geography teacher, Larissa Ivanovna invites me—she insists upon it—to her *dacha*. Her husband is a retired professor, she says. Her daughter is a poet, her son-in-law too and Sima—dark-haired oh-so-quiet Sima—whom I teach has a way with words as well.

'Meet me at eleven o'clock at the exit from the metro station at Prospekt Prosveshchenia (Enlightenment),' says Sima.

I want Stuart to go too, but it's our misfortune that holidays never coincide: when the school is off, the Institute (that raggle-taggle band of students called in from the highways and byways to form a new Institute in the wake of the departure of the former student body) meets, and he has two Greek classes and a session on Romans chapter 6.

Sonia wants to meet me at 8.30 to go over the Gospel passages we have to cover with the sixth and eighth classes before Easter.

I leave in a heavy snowfall. Because it's Lent, and Holy Week is coming soon, I read in English the Stations of the Cross as I stand in the crowded metro. I read how Franciscan brothers and friends in Dorset kept Good Friday amidst budding trees and birdsong. This land of Russia is snowbound still, and amidst all the concrete of the city no birds sing. Only crows croak in our courtyard. The child slumped across his father's knee beside me travels his own Via Dolorosa. The women in the next metro station are women of Jerusalem indeed. This never-ending circuit, these downtrodden servitors of a failed regime, make their sorry Stations of the Cross every day...

I look around me at the usual crowd of grey-faced people herded together like sheep going to the market. When we finally go away for good, whatever future date that may be, the awful thing will be to think that this sad life is still continuing.

At Pioneer Station I had a half-hour wait before the escalator would take me up. Such is the flow of people into town that only the down escalators work at this time of the morning. I was still holding my little book and the man beside me asked, 'Do you speak English?'

This could be dangerous. I was trapped here for half an hour, but in fact the speaker turned out to be an athlete from Ecuador, and we struck up a lively conversation which turned people's attention to us as we chatted away. Luis has been studying here five years without a single visit home. 'My father is *stolyar*... you know, carpenter, like José Maria... We are eight, Jenny. I am in the middle.'

He was going back home in July, he said, flying to Holland and thence to Canada, to USA and south to Ecuador, and he didn't want to lose his Russian language or his contact with his friends.

Time passed so quickly I was quite sorry when the escalators ground into action. We rode up together, exchanged addresses... and parted. I felt cheered that the metropolis, like all the market-places of the world, can be a place of meeting, not simply alienation.

Sonia greeted me as warmly as ever—with the words: 'There are variations in the Gospel stories: we'll have to take account of this... And look,' she'd been studying a children's story Bible with pictures. 'There's not one but three figures on crosses... Who could these other people be?'

Sonia insisted on feeding me with fried-up vermicelli and

sausage (breaking Lent). Gone are the days when I didn't eat between meals. Here you fuel yourself for the next slog through the snow, the next slither over ice, the next log-jam on overcrowded buses. Fat may be a feminist issue in the West. Here it's a matter of survival. But young recruits to the Army are on average a kilo underweight and few people look well.

I rush off to keep my appointment with Sima at the top of the escalator, the usual place of rendezvous. She's carrying a bag. It isn't full, but it seems heavy. 'It's our tomcat,' she explains.

Her mother joins us and we head off, dodging lakes of puddles for the out-of-town bus. We talk about swimming in the Black Sea and meeting sharks. A man with ginger eyebrows passes, stares, looks back, comes back to us and says: 'I see you standing laughing. No one laughs in our country any more.'

He soon realises I'm a foreigner, and feels that explains it all. Foreigners can laugh here. 'Life isn't so raw for you,' he says. He's been a sailor and when he hears I'm from Scotland, says he's been to Edinburgh. He's a big man, gangly, a bit drunk, and Sima's mother Tonya soon sends him packing with a curt, 'That's enough, thanks.'

Although Dostoyevsky has noted that Russia always had a soft spot for a drunkard, Slavs, we've noticed, tend not to be friends of the disreputable or the down-and-out. Or even of one another. We've found it's difficult to get friends to mix with other friends. 'He's a fool,' one friend told us cheerfully after one such failed encounter. 'She's wily ...' Consequently, we find it difficult to get groups of friends to meet together. It's better, we've found, to invite people separately. However, I find someone I can talk to on the bus. Sitting on the side seat is a little toddler with runny eyes and a plastic toy. Neither of us speaks Russian perfectly and we get on fine as the bus lurches out past the final tower blocks, past tumbledown wooden houses. We're heading for a settlement with a Finnish name and, indeed, as the bus fills up with *baboushki* I wonder if I hear Finnish being spoken in its local Ingrian variety—but it's actually peasant Russian spoken without teeth!

The bus stops at a last uninviting stop and we all get out.

'What was the *baboushka* talking to you about?' Sima asks her mother.

'She wanted to know about the cat. She wanted me to take him out.'

'That's nice, that she was talking to you,' I said, naïvely.

'Nonsense,' Tonia laughs. 'People either say: "You shouldn't take a cat on a bus." Or else; "You shouldn't keep an animal in a bag".'

We immediately leave the road and head through trees, walking carefully over slippery tracks. There are plans to bring gas here—and major fears that it will spoil the countryside. At the moment, families use calor gas delivered by lorry. Or wood, sawn by themselves.

As we slither over the ice, a young Alsatian comes bounding towards us. It's Cora—the family dog. She leaps up and down, giving Sima and her mother a great welcome, and the cat goes spare inside the shopping bag.

We turn up a path. There are one or two other wooden houses here. And snow and trees. No green things in sight.

The family built the *dacha* in the sixties. 'It stood alone then,' they told me. 'Just one or two Finnish families and ourselves. They've gone now and the hillsides are being built over.'

However, some people don't have enough money to finish building.

'This man here.' Tonia pointed to a half-built house. 'He doesn't have money. The house has been like that for three years. He's doing it himself, with his own hands. But that house there—that man's got money. It sprung up almost overnight.'

They had a two-storeyed house. The entrance was round the back, up a few steps into a passage, through two double doors. All the rooms were built around the stove, so you went through one room to get into the next, as Granny Larissa Ivanova explained as she welcomed me. She didn't stop for breath, and didn't stop talking all day, so much so that she forgot to put the tea in the pot when we finally sat down in the kitchen. She's an amateur artist, and the place was hung with her paintings of Crimea, of scenes through her window.

'My husband's gone shopping. All this place needs to be done up. But who's to do it? My husband's older than me. He's been ill. But he won't go to doctors. He just starves himself and does physical exercises. We got the doctor to him last winter—he had pneumonia and the only way we saved him, Tonia and I, was to give him injections. But he was furious with us...'

Professor Yuri Andreevich arrived, a gentle, white-haired man, silent, hard of hearing. Larissa Ivanovna more than made up for the rest of them. And so did four-year-old Katya, a little sister I didn't know Sima had.

'This tea has herbs in it. Mint. And...' Larissa named another herb I didn't know. 'It cures cancer. A friend of mine heard about it from an old granny who knew about these things. I always add it to tea.'

We ate fresh bread and blackcurrant pies made by Larissa. We heard how she and Yuri Andreevich have to stay here all winter to protect the house from thieves. Robbers have broken into their home in the Crimea and Larissa is about to make the long train journey south to see what has been stolen.

'But we've nothing to steal.'

Yuri Andreevich saws logs to feed the stove. They have tap water here, and calor gas in bottles. Their inside toilet is frozen over. They show me down the garden to their outside one. The door is off and they all tactfully withdraw.

I feel I should write a poem to that little place. Among the water closets of the world this one deserves a mention, though it has no water. Perhaps I felt so warm about it—though it was not a warm place—because here at last I was on my own. With nature, as Russians and Finns love to be, in more ways than one. It was clean and simple, a little shelter, open (by virtue of its missing door) to the sounds of a dog barking, to the bare trees— where no birds yet sang—to the hill behind, with one smaller wooden house, mercifully boarded up. Perhaps the family will manage to find hinges to mend the door before summer visitors come.

'I voted for Yeltsin,' Larissa Ivanovna says.

'I didn't,' her husband puts in.

'I know things are better than they were. My mother and I used to turn up the radio and whisper behind our hands when we wanted to speak. A friend of mine was a ballet dancer. They have to retire early, of course. A high-placed person, one of *them*, asked if she'd mind doing some cleaning. They paid well, and they gave her entry into shops she'd never dreamt of. She was shopping once, and there was another door. It was locked. There was nothing marked on it, it seemed an ordinary door. But, once, she saw inside. There was food there—like the supermarkets we hear of in the West. And cheap! So much cheaper than the State shops. That's how *they* lived. But we never saw it...'

That story about the shops sounds familiar. Perhaps it's apocryphal.

Larissa Ivanovna, Sima, little Katya and I go for a walk. Or rather we three walk and Katya rides on the sledge. Our path winds beside a lake and then into the forest. We look for good places to sledge. Soon the silent woods ring with our laughter as we tilt over ruts and our boots fill with snow.

Russians, who have such a horror of getting cold, don't mind tumbling around in snow. Last week I looked through the windows of Sonia's kitchen to see a heavy snowfall—a blizzard, to my way of thinking. So I said: 'I can't go just yet. It's snowing.' Sasha stared at me in disbelief. 'You won't melt,' he said.

Sledging is fantastic but I baulk at a particularly steep slope. 'I'm scared,' I say, to their amazement.

Our path takes us to where they're planning to build a railway line. All this forest area is under threat from redevelopment. Pylons already stride across a forest clearing. We walk under electric wires which hummed eerily. I pick pussy willow. But there are no green buds opening on the trees. Only, in the house, some birch twigs on the table have begun to unfurl tiny crinkled leaves. The cry of seagulls echoes through the bare trees.

Soon the woods will be alive with the sound of melting snow.

Paths will become cascading waterfalls. Roads turn to mud. The Great Melt, as Stuart—whose English has long since become Russian—puts it, will begin.

We walk through a birch grove. Naked, tall, the slender trees stretched their white trunks above us to the sky. Many have been milked, literally. Their silvery sides are scarred with square patches where their juice was taken last spring. And drunk.

'There's a wonderful power here,' says Larissa. 'Don't you feel it? Stand against the trees like this, look.' And she stands, rubbing herself against the nearest birch tree, but for me the power lies in the silent beauty of the trees stretching up to the still sky. Flakes of snow are starting to fall again, silver stars. Larissa, embracing one of the slender trees, is silent at last.

Not so the little granddaughter, crying because she does not want to walk through the deep snow and her feet are wet. 'Baba Jaga, the wicked witch, will get you,' says Larissa.

'I'll get her first,' Katya says, but Granny is no longer listening. She has already settled herself on the sledge and goes whooshing off home across the snow.

The stove is lit and we put our wet things around it. We eat soup made from salted carrots and onions Larissa prepared last autumn. There are two pieces of meat in mine and I eat, not wanting to refuse, knowing no one else has any. Our next course is lettuce, cucumber and the last of the pickled mushrooms. 'They grow all together at the foot of the tree, clustered close to the trunk,' says Larissa.

I would probably have called them toadstools.

And then we sing. Larissa is a trained singer. She gets down her guitar. For my sake she sings 'Coming through the Rye' in Russian. And a Scottish melody (unknown to me) reworked by Beethoven. I brought Scots songs too: 'The Skye Boat Song', 'Ye banks and braes', 'My love is like a red, red rose...'. 'Leave us the music. We'll copy them out.'

They give me stones from the Crimea, chalcedony and agate. Yuri shows me a grey stone. It has a fossil on it, a million years old, he says. They give me stones of a different sort as well, for cleansing the water. (One will sit in our water jar. We must wait three days for it to do its work.)

I travel back with Tonia. We are lucky... a bus is just about to leave. They live in a communal flat. It used to belong to the family, but it has been taken over by neighbours. The walls are thin. They can hear everything. 'We've been to the town council. They say, yes it's ours and by right we should be able to to buy back these other rooms. By right...'

But those words mean nothing. So now she and her husband are trying to scrape together $15,000 to buy forty square metres— a two-room apartment with its own kitchen and bathroom in an old flat in the centre of town which is being divided into two.

'Why doesn't your mother sell some of her paintings?' I wonder.

'She did, after her last exhibition. She sold two in Moscow. But you know it's not the done thing. Younger artists sell their work nowadays, but she's not used to it. It used to be, you'd ask someone to get something for you and you'd give them one of your paintings. She wouldn't know what price to ask. But, I'm sorry, here's my stop...'

She gets off, and I travel on home, glad of my day out in the country, glad of the snow and the birchwoods, glad of a quiet, unspoilt place.

THE ADVENT OF SPRING

28

Easter Song

Easter Eve—Russian style—and sunshine at last, with more than a hint of warmth in it, though there's not the slightest sign of green on any of the trees.

I went out this morning without a scarf over my head, wearing shoes instead of boots, a lighter coat. Flower sellers were standing outside the metro. The jazz band outside the hotel was in full swing—sound and colour amidst swirling dust. The snow has gone.

Along Nevsky Prospekt: the sound of loudspeakers; a procession carrying red flags, the hammer and sickle, slogans—'All Power to the Soviets'—chanting—Len-*in*-grad, Len-*in*-grad. A few people gathered along the kerb to watch; others shouted some sort of response which I didn't pick up. Someone said, with noticeable relief, 'Hardly anyone's taking part.'

The procession disappeared, and life went on as usual. I tackled the state shops, with their annoying, time-consuming business of queueing at the checkout to pay and then having to push your way back to the counter to pick up tomatoes or apples, butter or sausage—unwrapped, of course.

The free enterprise shop, by contrast, is clean, overstaffed. Smiling girls, each with her name stitched to her blouse—personalized service—asked if they could help. A bright Natasha put four boxes of (Dutch) fruit tea bags (at just under $1 a box) into a polythene bag for me, said, 'Goodbye and all the best.' She won't want all power to go back to the Soviets.

The tea is for me to take as presents this Sunday—Orthodox Easter.

Out in the bright sunshine I noticed that St Petersburg seems to be getting a face lift. Buildings are being repainted. Some shops are being given an attractive façade. Two new cafés have opened along Old Nevsky, and the road is being tarmacadamed. Steam-rollers are working with great gusto.

They are moving the beggars and street sellers too. There are far fewer now on the pavements and underpasses, though there's a noticeable police presence around the metro station entrances.

In fact at one metro station I saw the slumped figure of a middle-aged drunk, too blotto to move. A young policeman was trying to urge him on, but the man was too far gone to understand. The policeman started beating him with his truncheon. He seemed even more bewildered than the drunk whose coat I fancy was too thick, and the alcohol too overwhelming, for the blows to penetrate.

If the city is getting a spring-clean, so are we! Thursday of Orthodox Holy Week saw me moving Stuart out! We've asked if we could have a third room, the next one along the corridor, with a south-facing view like our own. I spent the day reorganizing our working places, and how good it is not to have Greek grammars among the toast and marmalade. All Thursday evening the bells rang for the solemn service, the Reading of the Gospels. We wanted to go, but the chance for getting work done in our new, more spacious surroundings simply couldn't be missed.

On Orthodox Great Friday, I'm sorry to say, we went to the theatre, not to church. Sonia had brought tickets. You are never asked beforehand. Friends phone and say: 'We're going to the theatre tonight.' But Sonia had been to church, for the first time ever on Good Friday, and when we met in the evening she was caught up in it all. The priest in their little wooden church had read the Gospel so clearly that even Vladik had understood. Christ is buried. Everyone venerates his coffin.

The 'yeast of the Kingdom' had obviously raised Sonia as high as the dough for the Easter *kulich* she was making for the first time—which she said had taken off and overflowed its dish.

The theatre bookstalls had the usual mess of cheap science fiction, mystery, lurid thrillers, pornography. However, Stuart found a novel about Peter the Great, and Sonia and I found a prayer book, together with memoirs written by people who had known the murdered priest Alexander Men, and a book of his sermons. Where else do you buy sermons in the theatre?

The acting and stage direction were brilliant, but I didn't enjoy the nineteenth-century comedy about a clerk who decided to die in order to live. He staged his funeral, took another name, and was put into prison where General Barabbas reinstated him by trickery. In the end the company bowed before a portrait of the Tsar, whose head slewed round to show a face grimacing with sardonic laughter.

However, tonight, like many other people, we shall crowd into church at midnight to hear the shout: 'Christ is risen, he is risen indeed!' burst out of darkness, dispersed by a mass of candles.

We set off at 11p.m. It's a mere five-minute walk to the Alexander Nevsky Church.

Crowds of people are standing outside. The church itself is in semi-darkness, the women's choir in their places on the balcony behind, but silent. An unseen priestly voice endlessly reads something totally incomprehensible to us and to the crowd packing into the great nave of the cathedral church. Young people crowd close, some just come because it's the fashion (though almost already becoming not the fashion again), others with slim, unlit candles; girls with covered heads. The couple jammed in front are cuddling, his head bent low, hers snuggling into his shoulder. The man beside me is drunk, and has the advanced stages of a smoker's cough, snorting, occasionally thumping out at the younger woman with him, unwashed and uncovered, wiping his snuffles into her collar. She endures it silently, only out of the corner of my eye I see the hard face she turns towards him.

On the other side—dim forms in the dark—I glimpse the patient old, the *baboushki*, and one old man. Are they kneeling? Or have they perhaps brought small wooden folding stools with them? They will have been in church for the readings from the Gospels on Thursday, for the solemn burial of the Lord on Friday, for the Sabbath stillness of the tomb today, and now they wait, fasting, among the noisy young, the curious, the foreigners...

I start to steam inside my coat. Stuart leans against me, rocking on his feet as crowds push him from behind, eyes closed, trying to endure. Somehow a way is thrust through the centre of the building, preparing for the Procession of the Cross at midnight. 'Move back,' we are ordered. 'Where to?' my noisy neighbour demands. 'We'll squash the *baboushki*.' There is a ripple of laughter, but the mood is neither light nor prayerful.

And still we wait and still more people crowd in.

Television crews get busy. There is a sizzling noise. I see people lighting candles, dipping each wick into their neighbour's flame; but the yellow pools of candleshine are obliterated by the white glare of television lighting. Prayers begin, the words chanted through loudspeakers by two disembodied male voices. There is no room to make the threefold sign of the cross, touching forehead and body, right shoulder, left shoulder with the thumb, first and middle finger of the right hand, to bow low from the waist. But a few heads bow, a few hands are raised in the incense swirls as banners and icons dip through the church. Priests and boys carry Christ's cross out into the darkness where people crowd, guarded by soldiery and police, among dark trees and crumbling quiet graves. A murmur of wonder ripples through the crowded church. Voices waver a hymn. I catch the words: 'With pure heart, Thee we praise.' But few of the young people round us know the words.

The first lights are lit. Television lighting picks out the wedding-cake-icing white of the baroque domed ceiling of this, one of the earliest St Petersburg churches. The choir on their balcony wait, like warriors leaning on their spears in the lull of battle. A long night lies ahead for them.

We shift, crushed, weary. In the silence voices sound: unrehearsed, untrained, but true. No angel voices these, but singing swelling from patient, maybe even holy hearts. 'With pure heart, Thee we praise... 'With pure heart... praise...' The *baboushki* are singing their hymn.

No angel voices—but the voices of Russia. Voices which endure. It is not the church hierarchy, mostly remote from the people, tarnished and compromised, but generations of grandmothers who have kept the faith alive. It was they who took the children of Communism secretly to church, taught them the prayers, showed them the icons, had them baptized. They kept the fasts, baked the Easter bread, passed on the recipes; they hid icons and crosses under bed-settees in communal flats; they said their prayers. They suffered through the bitter, hungry years of war, starving so that grandchildren could eat, weeping as they buried their dead. Their faith kept churches open. They had nothing to lose in the old regime; they have nothing to gain from this. Those four packets of tea I bought earlier cost almost as much as they have to feed themselves for a month.

They alone in the crowded church know the correct thing to do. They sing their hymn.

The processsion returns through the open doors of the church and the triumphant cry rings out: 'Christ is risen!' Hundreds of voices shout back: 'Truly risen!' So the young of Russia echo the ancient Easter message. Do they shout with their hearts? Already, having seen the 'show', people start to leave, but more are coming, and perhaps they are the ones who truly should have been here. A hand touches my arm. I turn. A young man in a wheelchair is being pushed through to the front. People make way for him and again the shouts resound: 'Christ is risen: He is risen indeed!' The voices of the choir resound round the white domes of the Cathedral, spilling out through loudspeakers to the crowds waiting outside amidst the glow, not of candles, but of lighted cigarettes, as the military in fur hats and heavy winter coats keep guard.

People start to drift home to party the night away. The *baboushki* will stay on till dawn, their wavering voices as ineffectual as candleshine in the white glare of electric lighting.

The testimony of those who watch and pray, of those who

count for nothing, is the very rock on which the church is founded—the rock whose name was given to Peter, the patron of this city, which will never fall apart, 'and the gates of hell will not prevail against it'.

His face is crowned with candleshines,
solemnity of soaring voices,
the incense word: pomiluj.
He is slumped in dust of five million trampling feet,
hat of rabbit fur askew.
Out of town we glimpse him among birches—
those naked Russian darlings—
reaching from thawing earth to distant blue.
Dark pines praise him,
bowed beneath April snow.
He is in the faces
of shawled women,
whose eyes suffer, bloodshot, bruised.
As well as in laughter of lovers
and children, swaddled like bundles
in soulless cities, shabby and subdued.